Instructor's Manual
for
The World of the Counselor
An Introduction to the Counseling Profession
Second Edition

Ed Neukrug
Stephanie Stone
Debra Boyce
Old Dominion University

Australia • Canada • Mexico • Singapore • Spain • United Kingdom • United States

Printed in the United States of America
1 2 3 4 5 6 7 05 04 03 02 01

Printer: Edwards Brothers

0-534-54966-7

For more information about our products, contact us at:
Thomson Learning Academic Resource Center
1-800-423-0563

For permission to use material from this text, contact us by:
Phone: 1-800-730-2214
Fax: 1-800-731-2215
Web: http://www.thomsonrights.com

Asia
Thomson Learning
5 Shenton Way #01-01
UIC Building
Singapore 068808

Australia
Nelson Thomson Learning
102 Dodds Street
South Street
South Melbourne, Victoria 3205
Australia

Canada
Nelson Thomson Learning
1120 Birchmount Road
Toronto, Ontario M1K 5G4
Canada

Europe/Middle East/South Africa
Thomson Learning
High Holborn House
50/51 Bedford Row
London WC1R 4LR
United Kingdom

Latin America
Thomson Learning
Seneca, 53
Colonia Polanco
11560 Mexico D.F.
Mexico

Spain
Paraninfo Thomson Learning
Calle/Magallanes, 25
28015 Madrid, Spain

CONTENTS

Introduction to Instructor's Manual

Although a survey course can be taught in many different ways, in this instructor's manual I will share my thoughts and how to teach "Introduction to Counseling" or an equivalent course that might use the text *The World of the Counselor*. Hopefully, you will find some of the things I do helpful. Of course, I would encourage you to adapt the book to your style of teaching. Therefore, you might want to stress certain chapters and not emphasize others.

The text presents an overview of the counseling profession by offering relevant content, vignettes, and think pieces for students to ponder. This book loosely follows the common-core curriculum standards of the Council for Accreditation of Counseling and Related Programs (CACREP), which include: (1)Human Growth & Development, (2) Helping Relationships, (3) Social & Cultural Foundations, (4) Group Work, (5) Career & Lifestyle Development, (6) Appraisal, (7) Research & Program Evaluation, and (8) Professional Orientation. The text also offers specific content in the specialty areas of Community Agency Counseling, School Counseling, and Student Affairs Practice (counseling in higher education settings). Having the text adhere to the CACREP-accredited common-core areas assures compliance with a high standard in the profession and offers the student a broad knowledge base. For this reason, the book could eventually be used as a source book and as a review for certification or licensing exams.

In recent years there has been rising interest in multicultural issues and in ethical, professional, and legal issues in counseling. Because I believe these issues are crucial to how we define our profession as we move into the 21st century, I have paid particular attention to them throughout the text. Thus, separate chapters provide information on ethical and professional Issues (Chapter 3), and on multicultural counseling (Chapters 14 and 15). In addition, at the end of each chapter I have included a focus on multicultural counseling and on ethical, professional, and legal issues. Finally, with my belief that each counselor should be a reflective person, I have concluded each chapter with a section entitled *The Counselor in Process* which stresses how the self-reflective counselor might deal with issues related to the chapter content.

The book is separated into seven sections. I have attempted to weave all of the eight common-core areas listed above into the first six sections of the text, with the seventh section focusing on the student's future in the counseling profession. The following offers some general teaching tips followed by a very brief overview of the seven sections of the text with some additional pedagogical suggestions.

General Teaching Goals

In a typical 15 week semester long course, I would recommend spending about two weeks on each section. It has been my experience that in a course like this many professors spend more time on one section or another, often spending an extended amount of time on counseling theories and counseling skills. I would strongly discourage this as I believe this detracts from all of the rich material in the rest of the text, and indeed, in the rest of our profession. Of course, I respect your individual teaching styles and hope you adapt the book to your way of teaching.

Because the content of a course like this is extensive, I would encourage you to *not* lecture from the material in the book. To do so would take much time, and generally students do not like such a dry approach. Instead, I would recommend that students be given an assignment of developing questions from the readings which could be responded to in class. To facilitate a direction for the class, I would suggest using the overheads of the chapters available for you at the end of this instructor's manual. Students could then add comments or ask their questions as you present the outline–without lecturing. In essence, you would be relying on the students to teach one another, with the instructor being an expert resource person. In addition, I would strongly urge you to intermingle experiential exercises such as those found in the companion workbook, *Experiencing the world of the counselor: A workbook for counselor educators and students*. You might want to assign segments out of the workbook prior to each class so students will be prepared for activities when they come to class. Also, remember, that at the end of each chapter multicultural issues, and ethical, professional, and legal issues are highlighted. Make sure some time is spent on these issues in every class. Finally, at the end of this instructor's manual is a sample syllabus which I have used to teach this course in the past. Feel free to use it, modify it, or discard it.

Section I: Professional Orientation

The name of this section reflects the CACREP common-core curriculum guideline of the same name, "Professional Orientation." Three chapters in this section include, Chapter 1: The Counselor's Identity: What, Who, and How?, Chapter 2: A History of the Counseling Profession, and Chapter 3: Standards in the Profession: Ethics, Accreditation, and Credentialing.

Teaching Concerns: This section begins with an analysis of the counseling profession. I have found that some students do not have a basic understanding of the differences among mental health professionals. Chapter 1 highlights these differences. Chapter 2 presents the history of the counseling profession, and also presents brief histories of the related professions of social work, psychology, and psychiatry. This helps place our profession in perspective. A chapter on history is typically dry, and I encourage you to intermingle experiential exercises that will pique students' interest. The last chapter in this section presents information on ethics, accreditation, and credentialing. Typically, students know little about the accreditation process or the credentialing process, and it is particularly important that students learn about these standards in our profession. Ethics is always fun to teach; however, I encourage you not to get caught up in spending too much time on this section of the chapter. Discussion about ethical issues can overwhelm the rest of the chapter.

***Section II: The Helping Relationship I:* Theory and Skills**

Section II loosely follows the CACREP common-core curriculum guideline entitled, "Helping Relationships," although consultation, which is listed under this CACREP guideline, is covered in Section III. The two chapters in this section are: Chapter 4: Individual Approaches to Counseling and Chapter 5: Counseling Skills.

Teaching concerns: Counseling theories, which are presented in Chapter 4, are always fun to discuss with the class. However, as noted earlier, this chapter can take over the course. I encourage you to focus the class on the highlights of this chapter so the material in the rest of the book does not get short-changed. Rather than presenting detail on a number of theories, I have chosen instead to examine four broad conceptual frameworks: psychodynamic, existential-humanistic, behavioral, and cognitive. Within each of these perspectives, I present one theory in a moderate amount of detail and also provide information on two or three other theories that fit into this perspective. At the end of this chapter I offer my view on how to develop an integrative (eclectic) approach to counseling. I also offer an overview of brief-treatment and solution-focused therapies. Have fun with this chapter. Discuss, role-play, argue, but don't get bogged down.

The counseling skills chapter in this section is another chapter in which one can get bogged down. I encourage you to do role-playing and to get students to role-play the skills in the chapter. It is equally important, however, that students understand about case conceptualization. So leave some time for this important topic.

<u>Section III: The Helping Relationship II: The Counselor Working in Systems</u>

This section draws from a number of CACREP curriculum guidelines which address counseling within systems, including: marriage and family counseling (from CACREP specialty guidelines called "Marriage and Family Counseling"), group work (from CACREP common-core curriculum guideline "Group Work"), and consultation and supervision (drawn from CACREP common-core curriculum guideline, "Helping Relationships"). The three chapters in this section are Chapter 6: Family Counseling, Chapter 7: Group Work, and Chapter 8: Consultation and Supervision.

Teaching concerns: The most challenging part of this section for me is helping students see the connection among the content in these three chapters. Systemic thinking can be challenging to students who have thought linearly. Having students see the connections among people in families, people in groups, people in organizations, and among the client, supervisor and supervisee is exciting. These three chapters lend themselves toward class role-play, and I encourage you to have fun finding experiential exercises that will help students see the world in a contextual manner.

<u>Section IV: Development of the Person</u>

This section examines the broad spectrum of human development issues in counseling. Loosely following two of the CACREP common-core curriculum guidelines of Human Growth and Development, and Career and Lifestyle Development, this section includes Chapter 9: Development Across the Lifespan, Chapter 10: Abnormal Development, Diagnosis, and Psychopathology, and Chapter 11: Career Development: The Counselor and the World of Work

Teaching concerns: My major concern about this section is the controversy that still exists in our profession and in society about what is "normal" and what is "abnormal." I believe it is critical for students to understand that the concept of normality is a social construction, and I would encourage you to have students become actively involved in heated discussion about these concepts. They'll love it.

I have included in the section on abnormal development an overview of the DSM-IV-TR and of psychotropic medications. I believe this may be controversial; however, I can no longer see counselors doing their job effectively without some knowledge of these areas. Obviously, if you disagree, you can always skip over this section. I hope you don't.

For the chapter on career development I believe it's important to show this chapter's developmental connection to the other chapters in this section. Therefore, as the profession has moved toward a developmental notion of career, I hope that you reflect this in the way you present the chapter. Of course, the content in this chapter lends itself to some fun experiential exercises.

Section V: Research, Program , Evaluation, and Appraisal
This section is based on two CACREP common-core curriculum guidelines: Research and Program Evaluation, and Appraisal. The two chapters in this section include Chapter 12: Testing and Assessment, and Chapter 13: Research and Evaluation

Teaching concerns: For over twenty years I have taught testing, and I am still amazed that so many people think this area is dry. Similarly, research and evaluation can also be made to be exciting. Have fun with this section. Show some projective tests, discuss the horrors of testing. Discuss the positives of testing. Give outrageous examples of research studies. Have students develop research studies. Indeed, if we present this in a dry way, students will leave this class expecting it to be boring later. If you need some ways to make this section spicier, use some of the exercises from the companion workbook.

Section VI: Social and Cultural Foundations in Counseling
This section loosely follows the CACREP common-core curriculum guideline of the same name, Social and Cultural Foundations in Counseling. The two chapters included in this section are Chapter 14: Theory and Concepts of Multicultural Counseling, and Chapter 15: Knowledge and Skills of Multicultural Counseling.

Teaching concerns: I purposely gave multicultural issues its own section with two chapters. I believe that multicultural counseling is the most crucial topic for counselors to understand today. With so few counselors and counselor educators of color, and with so many minority individuals not attending counseling or having horrible experiences in counseling, we must ensure that our students leave our programs with a strong understanding of other cultures and with the basic ability to understand people from other cultures.

The balance for me in a section like this is helping students both learn the content and learn about themselves. Finding the right mix of lecture, discussion, feedback, and sharing is indeed an art. The chapters in this section are divided into theory and skills. Thus, I would encourage you to first discuss theory, as a backdrop. Such a foundation makes it easier to discuss the skills needed to work with people from different cultures and sets the stage for students to do some personal self-reflection. Finally, experiential exercises in the area of social and cultural issues abound, and if used effectively, can offer in-depth learning and increased self-awareness. However, if used poorly, they can lead to hostility and mistrust on the part of the student.

Section VII: Your Future in the Counseling Profession: Choosing a Specialty Area, Finding a Job, and Trends in the Future
This last section of the text begins with an examination of the three most popular specialty areas in counseling: School Counseling, Community Agency/Mental Health Counseling, and Student Affairs Practice (Counseling in a Higher Education Setting). Each of these chapters provides history, defines roles and functions, presents theory and practice issues, and provides the student with specific examples of what it's like to work in each of these specialty areas. Places of potential employment and approximate salaries are also given. This section ends with a chapter that examines trends in the future of the counseling profession. It includes a segment that examines job and/or graduate program choices in the student's future.The section includes Chapter 16: School Counseling, Chapter 17: Community Agency Counseling and Mental Health Counseling, Chapter 18: Student Affairs Practice in Higher Education, and Chapter 19: A Look Toward the Future.

Teaching concerns: This section both marks the end of the course and talks about the future of the student as well as the future of the profession. Although many students know which specialty area in counseling they would like to pursue, others are unsure. This section gives a fairly detailed analysis of three of the more popular specialty areas in the profession: agency/mental health counseling counseling, school counseling, and student affairs practice (college counseling). In teaching this course, I have had students break up into groups early in the semester based on the specialty area which they think they would like to pursue. I then ask students in each of the three groups to present one-half of a class on that specialty area. I encourage them to outline the chapter in the book and to intermingle their presentation with experiential exercises. This allows students to feel a part of their specialty area while learning about it. It is also a method of developing cohort groups in students' specialty areas.

Finally, Chapter 19 offers some trends in the profession as we move through the 21st century. Discuss these, have students offer other ideas, and have fun. Also in this chapter you will find some information about going to graduate school and getting a job. While many students have already decided on their graduate school plans, some may not have. In addition, most students will be interested in some basic information about obtaining a job. As you near the end of this chapter keep in mind that the class is coming to an end. You might consider using the theme of "looking toward the future" as a mechanism for saying good-bye and providing closure to the class.

Student Resources

Please note that multiple choice questions marked with "www" will available as an online quiz under student resources at www.wadsworth.com. In addition, at the conclusion of each chapter in the instructor's manual you will find a list of key words that can be used to research topics through INFOTRAC.

EXAM QUESTIONS

CHAPTER 1

WHO IS THE COUNSELOR? WHAT IS COUNSELING?

Multiple Choice

1. Which of the following best defines the term guidance (pp. 3-4)? (www)
   a. Shorter term, surface issues, here and now, preventive, conscious
   b. Long-term, personality construction, deep-seated issues, unconscious
   c. Psychoeducational, group work, family oriented, past
   d. All of the above

2. The difference between guidance, counseling, and psychotherapy can be seen as (pp. 3-5):
   a. substantial
   b. nonexistent
   c. a matter of degree, with counseling being somewhere in-between
   d. not important

3. The accreditation body for counseling programs is (p. 5): (www)
   a. the Council for the Accreditation of Counseling and Related Educational Programs
   b. the National Board of Certified Counselors
   c. the American Psychological Association
   d. the National Accreditation Counseling Association

4. CORE is the accreditation body for (p. 5):
   a. community counseling programs
   b. rehabilitation counseling programs
   c. counseling in organizational environment programs
   d. All of the above

5. Which is true about licensed professional counselors (p. 5)?
   a. They can often obtain third-party reimbursement
   b. They are generally licensed by the specific state in which they work.
   c. They are usually licensed by the National Board for Certified Counselors
   d. a and b
   e. a and c

6. Which of the following is *not* a specialty area as recognized by CACREP (p. 6-7)?
   a. School counseling
   b. Marriage and family counseling
   c. Mental health counseling
   d. Community counseling
   e. Gerontological counseling
   f. Rehabilitation counseling

7. Which association is mainly for psychologists (p. 7, 12)?
   a. APA b. ACA c. NOHSE d. NASW e. NAP

8. Which association is mainly for human service workers (p. 14)?
   a. NASW b. AHSA c. NOHSE d. HSWA e. ACA

9. Which association is mainly for psychiatric nurses (p. 9, 13)?
   a. PNAA b. APNAA c. NAPP d. APNA

10. Which association is mainly for social workers (p. 8, 13)? (www)
    a. NASW b. ASWA c. NSWA d. ACSWE

11. Which association is mainly for psychiatrists (p. 8, 13)?
    a. APA b. ACA c. NOHSE d. NASW e. NAP

12. Which of the following can never write prescriptions (p. 8)?
   a. Psychologists
   b. Psychiatrists
   c. Psychiatric Nurses
   d. a and c
   e. None of the above can write prescriptions

13. What is one major role of school psychologists (p. 8)?
   a. To do counseling in the schools
   b. To provide advice on medication for learning disabilities
   c. To offer ways of administrating new innovative counseling programs
   d. To test children in the schools

14. Which is ***not*** true of psychiatric nurses (p. 9)?
   a. They have little or no training in mental health counseling
   b. In the majority of states, they can write prescriptions
   c. They can become certified on the bachelor's or master's level
   d. None of the above (all are true)

15. Sexton (1993, Sexton & Whiston, 1991; 1994) highlighted the fact that research on the effectiveness of counseling shows that (p. 14)?
   a. as many individuals improve over time without counseling as compared to those who are in counseling
   b. counseling is only slightly more effective than not being in counseling
   c. the vast majority of individuals improve in counseling
   d. counseling effectiveness cannot be measured

16. In reference to the counseling, genuineness is (p. 15-16):
   a. authenticity in the helping relationship
   b. realness in the helping relationship
   c. a quality that effects all helping relationships
   d. all of the above

17. An empathic person is one who has (p. 15):
   a. experienced the problem of another person
   b. dealt with that kind of problem before
   c. been certified as being empathic
   d. the ability to understand another's problem as if it was their own
   e. All of the above

18. People who are accepting of others (p. 16): (www)
   a. condone everything a person does
   b. accept people unconditionally
   c. accept people in their differences
   d. All of the above
   e. b and c only

19. Open-minded people who are nondogmatic (p. 16-17):
   a. allow others to express their points of view
   b. do not have strong views
   c. allow others to express their points of view and subtly try to change others to their point of view
   d. tend to be more empathic than those who are dogmatic and close-minded
   e. Two of the above
   f. Three of the above

20. Mindful people are people who (p. 17-18):
   a. heavily rely on others to make decisions
   b. are focused, sensitive, and contextual
   c. rely more on self than others for decision-making
   d. rarely, if ever, ask for the opinions of others
   e. Two of the above
   f. Three of the above

21. While many counselor attributes are related to client outcomes, one attribute that seems to be the most strongly related is (p. 19):
   a. being empathic
   b. being nonjudgmental
   c. having an internal locus of control
   d. being good at building a counseling relationship
   e. being mentally healthy

22. *Joining* is a term used by Salvadore Minuchin which can be most associated with which of the following counselor attributes (19)?
   a. Empathy
   b. Being mentally health
   c. Acceptance
   d. Being good at building a counseling relationship
   e. Genuineness

23. Counselor competence includes all but which of the following (p. 19-20)?
   a. Having a thirst for knowledge
   b. Reading the professional literature
   c. Practicing only in one's specialty area
   d. Knowing when to consult with others
   e. Knowing one's limitations
   f. All of the above

24. Research on the well-adjusted counselor shows: (p. 18)
   a. they are more effective than those who are not well-adjusted
   b. mixed about their effectiveness
   c. they are less effective than counselors who are struggling with their issues
   d. none of the above

25. A constructive development perspective on the characteristics of the effective counselor suggests which of the following (p. 20)?
   a. Counselors at lower stages are likely to develop at slower rates that those at higher stages
   b. Counselor development is stagnant
   c. All counselors are capable of movement toward higher stages
   d. Developmental models are not as useful as pathological models in understanding why some counselors get stuck in lower stages of development

26. Perry and Kegan offer different theories of constructive development, however, both theories suggest all but which of the following (p. 20)?
   a. Development moves from lower to higher stages
   b. Development is sequential and predictable
   c. Counselors tend to move from concreted, rigid thinking to more abstract, flexible thinking
   d. Challenging counselors, without support, is critical for counselor growth and change

27. ACAs Human Concerns Fund (HCF) (p. 12):
   a. provides advocacy for counselors
   b. provides assistance for the needy
   c. is a organization for scrutinizing the ethics of research
   d. All of the above

28. Which of the following is *not* a membership benefit of ACA (p. 12)? (www)
   a. Professional development programs, such as conferences and continuing education workshops
   b. Counseling resources, such as books, video and audio tapes, and journals
   c. Computer assisted job search services
   d. Professional liability insurance
   e. Assistance in lobbying efforts at the local, state, and national levels
   f. Networking and mentoring opportunities
   g. Subscription to the *Journal of Counseling and Development* and other professional journals based on division membership
   h. A variety of discount and specialty programs (e.g., mastercard, air travel, and, so forth)
   i. None of the above (all are membership benefits)

29. The American Association of Marriage and Family Therapists (p. 13):
   a. is a division of ACA
   b. is a separate association from ACA
   c. shares few goals with IAMFC
   d. offers few, if any benefits to its members

30. The American Psychological Association was founded in 1892 by (p. 12):
   a. Minuchin b. Eysenck **c.** G. Stanley Hall d. E. G. Williamson

31. Clients from non-white backgrounds are (p. 21):
   a. likely to have mental illness at higher rates than whites
   b. likely to attend counseling at similar rates as whites
   c. likely to terminate counseling at higher rates than whites
   d. less likely to be misdiagnosed than whites
   e. None of the above

32. Relative to multicultural counseling, Whitfield suggests that (p. 21):
   a. each counseling graduate is multilingual
   b. each counseling graduate has a multicultural view
   c. each counseling graduate is multiculturally literate
   d. each counseling graduate is ethnically informed
   e. Two of the above
   f. Three of the above
   g. All of the above

True of False

33. Guidance is to Counseling as Counseling is to Psychotherapy (pp. 3-4) (T).

34. Most texts do not differentiate between the terms counseling and psychotherapy (p. 4) (**T**).

35. NBCC is the accrediting body for counselors (p. 5) (**F**).

36. All specialty areas in counseling tend to have the same basic foundational course work (p. 5) (**T**).

37. The training of psychologists and psychiatrists is very similar (pp. 7-8) (**F**).

38. Although one needs a doctorate to be a counselor or clinical psychologist, usually, only a master's degree is necessary to be a school psychologist (p. 5-8) (**F**).

39. Today, the differences between counseling and clinical psychology are great (p. 5-8) (**F**).

40. Neukrug's eight characteristics of the effective counselor are based on the current state of research in the field (p. 15) (**T**).

41. Social workers tend to have less training than counselors in the areas of careers, testing, and quantitative research (p. 9) (**T**).

42. Eysenck's research, which stated that approximately two-thirds of clients will improve on their own, has been shown to be accurate (pp. 14-15) (**F**).

43. Gelso and Carter (1994) suggest that the "real relationship" exists in every counseling relationship and needs to be acknowledged by the counselor if not by the client (p. 19) (**T**).

44. Research on cross-cultural personality styles shows that a high degree of internal locus of control is desirable in almost all cultures (p. 17) (**F**).

45. Most counselors have participated in their own counseling (p. 18) (**T**).

46. The mental health of the counselor has *not* been empirically shown to be related to client outcomes (p. 18) (**F**).

47. Countertransference is likely related to the mental health of the counselor (p.18) (**T**).

48. The identity of the counselor is closely related to knowing our boundaries and limitations (p. 21) (**T**).

49. Counselors should seek to refer only to individuals within their own profession in order to maintain continuity and protect the integrity of the profession (p. 21) (**F**).

Fill in the Blank (Questions 5067)

Below are the acronyms of the 15 divisions and one affiliate division of the American Counseling Association (ACA). Fill in their complete names in the space provided.(p. 11)

50. AAC______________________________
51. AADA______________________________
52. ACCA______________________________
53. ACEG______________________________
54. ACES______________________________
55. AGLBIC______________________________
56. AMCD______________________________
57. AMHCA______________________________
58. ARCA______________________________
59. ASCA______________________________
60. ASERVIC______________________________
61. ASGW______________________________
62. C-AHEAD______________________________
63. CSJ______________________________
64. IAAOC______________________________
65. IAMFC______________________________
66. NCDA______________________________
67. NECA______________________________

INFOTRAC KEY WORDS: Counselor characteristics. Impaired therapist. Professional associations.

CHAPTER 2

A HISTORY OF THE COUNSELING PROFESSION

Multiple Choice

1. The supreme court decision that led to the deinsitutionalization of the mentally ill was (p. 41):
   a. PL94-142 c. Miller vs. the U. S.
   b. Donaldson v. O'Connor d. Wagner O'Day Act

2. Which of the following did not affect the early beginnings of the counseling field (pp. 32-33)?
   a. The development of the first tests
   b. The development of psychoanalysis
   c. The social reform movements
   d. The development of new drugs to aid in the treatment of mental illness
   e. The Industrial Revolution

3. Which is not correctly matched: (pp. 46-47) (www)
   a. Hippocrates: Treatment of Mental Illness
   b. Plato: Interpretation of the Human Condition
   c. Augustine and Aquinas: Belief in the supernatural
   d. Socrates: Study of knowledge and objective reality

4. Which is not correctly matched: (pp. 46-47)
   a. Jane Addams: Hull House
   b. Charity Organization Societies: Friendly visitors
   c. Elizabethan Poor Laws: Institutionalization of the Poor
   d. None of the above (all are correctly matched)

5. Which of the following did not initiate guidance services in the schools at the turn of the century (pp. 34-35)?
   a. Eli Weaver b. Anna Reed c. Jesse Davis **d.** E. G. Williamson

6. Frank Parsons, (pp. 34-35):
   a. is considered by some the founder of guidance in America
   b. created a comprehensive theory of vocational guidance
   c. was concerned about humane methods of working with people
   d. developed concepts that greatly affected the broader field of counseling
   e. Two of the above
   f. Three of the above
   g. All of the above

7. Which act created the U. S. Employment Services and helped to spread vocational counseling (p. 35)?
   a. Wagner O'Day Act c. NDEA
   b. The Great Society Initiatives d. Manpower Development and Training Act

8. This individual was hospitalized for schizophrenia and later wrote a book on his experiences and advocated for the humane treatment of the mentally ill (p. 36). (www)
   a. John Brewer c. Dorothea Dix
   b. Benjamin Rush **d.** Clifford Beers

9. The trait and factor approach, as advocated by E. G. Williamson suggests which of the following (p. 38)?
   a. Analyze, synthesize, diagnose, counsel, follow-up
   b. Listen, understand, synthesize, counsel, suggest, follow-up
   c. Listen, understand, interpret, reflect, follow-up
   d. None of the above

10. Which was *not* true of E.G. Williamson (p. 38): (www)
   a. he developed one of the first comprehensive theories of counseling
   b. he was an early psychoanalyst that split from Freud's basic views
   c. he developed a trait and factor approach to counseling
   d. he had a 5-step counseling approach: analyzing, synthesizing, diagnosing, counseling, and follow-up

11. Carl Rogers' early approach to counseling was (p. 38):
   a. humanistic, client-centered, nondirective, relatively short-term, and humane
   b. affected greatly by the vocational guidance movement
   c. modeled after the basic tenets of Freudian psychoanalysis
   d. a reaction to the existential humanists who were having increasing influence in the United States

12. The National Defense Education Act (NDEA) did which of the following (p. 39)?
   a. Spread humanistic education and counseling methods throughout the country
   b. Supported compulsory education
   c. Gave money for the training of school counselors in an effort to identify potential scientists
   d. Gave money for education to returning GIs from World War II

13. Choose the progression that reflects the name changes of the American Counseling Association (p. 35, 39).
   a. ACPA⇨AAAMFT⇨AACD⇨ACA
   b. NVGA⇨APGA⇨AACD⇨ACA
   c. APGA⇨ACPA⇨NVGA⇨ACA
   d. NVGA⇨APGA⇨ACES⇨AACD⇨ACA

14. The Counseling Division of the American Psychological Association is (p. 39): (www)
   a. Division 1 b. Division 2 c. Division 17 d. The Counseling Division

15. Which ACA division was *not* formed during the 1950s (pp. 39-40)?
   a. ASCA b. ACES c. NCDA d. ARCA e. AHEAD
   f. None of the above: All were formed during the 1950s

16. For the counseling profession, the 1960s represented which of the following (pp. 39-40)?
   a. An era of increased diversification
   b. The passing of numerous social service acts that resulted in jobs for counselors
   c. The development of ethical guidelines
   d. The early beginnings of the accreditation movement
   e. Two of the above
   f. Three of the above
   g. All of the above

17. This initiative by President Lyndon Johnson provided most of the legislation which created the funding for many social service programs (p. 40).
   a. The creation of the National Institute of Mental Health
   b. Civil right legislation initiative
   c. The Great Society
   d. The Community Mental Health Centers Act

18. The Community Mental Health Centers Act of 1963 did all but which of the following (p. 40)? (www)
   a. Established mental health centers nationally
   b. Provided for outpatient, inpatient, emergency, partial hospitalization, and consultation and education services
   c. Offered vocational rehabilitation services for the poor
   d. Provided low-cost or free mental health services

19. Which ACA division was not formed during the 1960s (p. 42)?
   a. NECA b. ASGW c. AAC d. None of these (All were formed during the 1960s)

20. For the counseling profession, the 1970s was highlighted by (pp. 40-42):
    a. a decrease in the number of individuals seeking outpatient counseling
    b. an increase in the number of counselors who worked with individuals with disabilities
    c. the development of "microcounseling skills training"
    d. increased professionalism in the field
    e. Two of the above
    f. Three of the above
    g. All of the above

21. Which ACA division was not formed during the 1970s (p. 43)?
    a. AMCD b. ASGW c. IAAOC d. AMHCA **e.** ASCA
    f. None of the above (All were formed during the 1970s)

22. The 1980s to the present have stressed which of the following in the counseling profession (pp. 42-43)?
    a. The focus on client-centered counseling skills
    b. The development of new theoretical approaches to counseling
    c. The cutback on the number of counselors
    d. The proliferation of standards in the profession (e.g., ethical guidelines, accreditation, credentialing)

23. NBCC offers certification in which of the following areas (p. 43)?
    a. School counseling
    b. Clinical mental health counseling
    c. Approved clinical supervisor
    d. Addictions counseling
    e. Two of the above
    f. Three of the above
    g. All of the above

24. Which ACA division was not formed during the 1980s or 1990s (pp. 42-43)? (www)
    a. ACEG b. AADA c. IAMFC d. ACCA **e.** ASCA
    f. None of the above: All were formed during the 1980s or 1990s

25. In the past few years, the counseling profession has particularly emphasized all but which of the following (pp. 42-44)?
    a. A developmental focus in the training of counselors
    b. Multicultural counseling
    c. Standards of Practice
    d. A return to vocational guidance activities

True or False

26. The counseling profession shows a history that has continually focused on the issue of multicultural counseling (p. 45) **(F)**.

27. As a reflection of the stability of the profession, since the adoption of a code of ethics in 1961, ACA has revised its code of ethics only once (pp. 45, 48) **(F)**.

28. Aristotle is sometimes said to be the first psychologist (p. 46) **(T)** .

29. The humanistic psychology and education movement was greatly affected by philosophers fleeing Europe during World War II (p. 38) **(T)**.

30. Hippocrates believed that spirits were the cause of mental illness (p. 25) **(F)**

31. John Brewer was a colleague of Freud's who explored how hypnotism could be used to cure physical problems of psychological origin (p. 35) **(F)**.

32. The Army Alpha was a test of cognitive ability that was used to determine placements of recruits during World War I (pp. 36-37) **(T)**.

33. Woodworth's Personal Data Sheet was a test of cognitive ability that was used to determine placements of recruits during World War I (p. 36) **(F)**.

34. Dr. Benjamin Rush was known for his innovative treatment of the mentally ill (pp. 30-31) **(T)**.

35. Dorethea Dix established one of the first Charity Organization Societies in the U. S. (p. 27) **(F)**.

36. Today, few people see Freud's original theory as novel for its time(p. 29) **(F)**.

37. The American Psychological Association was founded at the end of the 19th century (p. 29) **(T)** .

38. Although the origins of the professions of counseling, psychology, social work, and psychiatry are very similar, today their roles are quite different (p. 26) **(F)** .

39. The origin of the social work movement was partially responsible for today's emphasis on a systems approach to understanding clients (pp. 27-28) **(T)**.

40. The concept of the separation of mind and body was a construction developed by early Christians and early philosophers (p. 26) **(T)**.

Pick the Correct Item (Items 41-49)

a. Psychiatry b. Psychology c. Social Work d. None of the above

From the list above, pick the item that impacted upon the counseling profession in the manner listed below and place the letter in the space provided.

41. ___Developed tests that were later used by counselors (**b**) (p. 30).

42. ___Developed research techniques that are now used by counselors (**b**) (p. 30).

43. ___Responsible for many early approaches to counseling that are still widely used today (**b**) (p. 29).

44. ___Developed a classification system of mental illness (**a**) (pp. 32).

45. ___Has provided a basis for understanding the psychobiology of mental illness (**a**) (p. 32).

46. ___Helped counselors understand clients from a systemic perspective (**c**) (pp. 27-28).

47. ___Gave counselors an awareness of the importance of advocacy with clients (**c**) (p. 28).

48. ___Provided a model for the importance of field experiences in the training of mental health professionals (**c**) (p. 28).

49. ___ Provided a detailed understanding of career counseling and vocational guidance (**d**).

Matching (pp. 46-47).

50.	___Wundt **(e)**	a. called by some the 1st psychologist
51.	___Socrates **(a)**	b. one of 1st to practice hypnosis
52.	___Binet **(d)**	c. developer of classical conditioning
53.	___Freud **(f)**	d. developed 1st modern intelligence test
54.	___Charcot/Mesmer **(b)**	e. one of 1st experimental psychologists
55.	___Pavlov **(c)**	f. 1st comprehensive theory of psychotherpay

INFOTRAC KEY WORDS: History of counseling. History of psychology. History of social work. History of psychiatry.

CHAPTER 3

STANDARDS IN THE PROFESSION: ETHICS, ACCREDITATION, AND CREDENTIALING

Multiple Choice

1. Morality is concerned with__________, ethics with__________(p. 51).
   a. conduct; the process of examining moral behavior
   b. process of examining moral behavior; conduct
   c. behavior; what is legal and illegal
   d. how we think about behavior; legal issues
   e. religion; the process of examining moral behavior

2. Ethical relativists believe that (p. 52): (www)
   a. ethical judgements should be based on universal truths
   b. any individual counselor can never come to any final decisions regarding ethical dilemmas
   c. ethical decision making is a process that can never be justified
   d. moral rules are culturally predominant preferences

3. "Murder can be justified under certain circumstances" would likely be stated by (p. 52):
   a. an ethical relativist
   b. a person who believes in the concept of universal truths
   c. a moralist
   d. a religious ethical, moralist

4. Some purposes of ethical codes include all but which of the following (p. 54)?
   a. To protect consumers and further the professional standing of the organizations.
   b. To serve "as a vehicle for professional identity and a mark of the maturity of the profession."
   c. To guide professionals toward certain types of behaviors that reflect the underlying values considered important for the professional group.
   d. To provide a professional a framework in the sometimes difficult ethical and professional decision-making process.
   e. Being a measure of defense in case the professional is sued for malpractice by offering a legal document that can support the professional's actions.

5. Some of the limitations of ethical codes include all but which of the following (p. 54)? (www)
   a. There are many issues that cannot be handled in the context of a code.
   b. Codes are often so rigid, that the professional finds himself or herself with few options.
   c. There is often no way to bring the interests of the client, patient, or research participant systematically into the code construction process.
   d. There are parallel forums in which the issues in the code may be addressed with the results sometimes at odds with the findings of the code (e.g., in the courts).
   e. There are possible conflicts between two codes, between the practitioner's values and code requirements, between the code and ordinary morality, between the code and institutional practice, and between requirements within a single code.

6. Which of the following sections is not included within the ACA code of ethics (pp. 54-55)?
   a. The counseling relationship
   b. Professional responsibility
   c. Relationships with other professionals
   d. Evaluation, assessment, and interpretation
   e. Teaching, training, and supervision
   f. Research and publication
   g. None of the above (the code speaks to each section)

7. Which of the following steps in the decision making model of Corey, et al. (1998) is out of sequence (p. 56)?
   a. Identify the problem and the potential issues involved
   b. Obtain consultation
   c. Review the relevant ethical guidelines
   d. Consider possible courses of action and enumerate their potential consequences
   e. Decide on what appears to be the best course of action

8. Which of the following did Kitchener (1984) *not* suggest (p. 56)?
   a. To promote *consensus value making* in ethical decision making
   b. To consider the *autonomy* of the client
   c. To consider the *beneficence* of society
   d. To assure *nonmaleficense* of people
   e. To be *just* and *fair*
   f. To show *fidelity* or *faithfulness*

9. Rest suggests that (pp. 56-57): (www)
   a. ethical decision making is a four-step process that begins with moral perceptions and ends with the decision
   b. one should gauge and select underlying moral principles in making ethical decisions
   c. ethical decision making is less of a moral than a spiritual process
   d. All of the above

10. Critiques of ethical decision making models include all but which of the following (p. 58)?
   a. They are not particularly sensitive to cross-cultural issues
   b. They do not emphasize the person behind the principles which they espouse
   c. They are too heavily based on moral principles
   d. They lean too heavily on legal issues

11. Cognitive developmental models of ethical decision making assume all of the following except (p. 58):
   a. lower level thinking is dualistic and rigid
   b. higher level thinking is abstract and flexible
   c. lower level and higher level thinkers could come to the same conclusions
   d. higher level thinkers are likely to rely more on ethical codes than lower level thinkers
   e. None of the above, all are correct

12. Below are listed some of the complaints made against LPCs as noted Neukrug, Milliken, & Walken (2001). Going from the most to the least number of complaints, which below represents the accurate representation of their findings (p. 60)?
   a. Having sex with a client, inappropriate fee assessment, inappropriate dual relationship, failure to inform clients about rules of relationship, breach of confidentiality, practicing without a license
   b. Inappropriate fee assessment, having sex with a client, inappropriate dual relationship, failure to inform clients about rules of relationship, breach of confidentiality, practicing without a license
   c. Inappropriate dual relationship, incompetence in the facilitation of a counseling relationship, practicing without a license, having a sexual relationship with a client, breach of confidentiality, inappropriate fee assessment, failure to inform clients about rules of relationship, failure to report abuse, failure to inform clients about rules of relationship, breach of confidentiality
   d. Having sex with a client, breach of confidentiality, failure to apply duty to warn, inappropriate fee assessment, inappropriate dual relationship, failure to inform clients about rules of relationship, breach of confidentiality

13. Which of the following would be an appropriate avenue to report ethical complaints (pp. 60-61)?
   a. State licensing board
   b. State professional association
   c. ACA ethics committee
   d. All of the above
   e. All except "c"

14. Which of the following does not offer accreditation (pp. 64-65)? (www)
   a. The Council on Rehabilitation Education (CORE)
   b. The American Association of Pastoral Counselors (AAPC)
   c. The American Psychological Association (APA)
   d. The Council on Social Work Education (CSWE)
   e. The Commission on Accreditation for Marital & Family Therapy EducatioN (COAMFTE)
   f. None of the above (all offer accreditation)

15. Of the accreditation bodies in question 14, which offer(s) a competing accreditation with CACREP (p. 65)?
   a. CORE
   b. AAPC
   c. APA
   d. CSWE
   e. COAMFTE
   f. CORE and APA
   g. CORE and COAMFTE
   h. CORE, APA, and COAMFTE

16. Which is incorrect (p. 61)?
   a. Civil liability is when one's actions leaves one open to a lawsuit brought by an individual or class of individuals.
   b. Criminal liability is when one's actions leaves one open to a lawsuit brought by the state or governing body.
   c. Counselors can be sued criminally or civilly
   d. a and b are both incorrect
   e. a, b, and c are all incorrect
   f. None incorrect (all are correct)

17. CACREP accreditation generally does all but which of the following (p 64)?
   a. Leads to better faculty and students
   b. Leads to better job opportunities
   c. Offers programs to creatively develop new programs that offer experimental courses, different curriculum guidelines, and different credit hours for the degree.
   d. Becomes the standards by which credentialing bodies determine who is eligible to become credentialed and generally assures higher overall standards of programs.
   e. None of the above (CACREP accreditation leads to all of the items listed)

18. Credentialing does all but which of the following (p. 66)? (www)
   a. Increases professionalism
   b. Helps counselors achieve parity with other professional associations
   c. Assures third-party reimbursement
   d. Helps to protect the public
   e. Helps counselors define who they are

19. Pick the item that correctly lists the three types of credentialing in their order of complexity (from lowest to highest) (pp. 66-67).
   a. Registration, licensure, certification
   b. Registration, certification, licensure
   c. Certification, registration, licensure
   d. Certification, licensure, registration
   e. Licensure, certification, registration
   f. Licensure, registration, certification

20. Which credential generally defines the title *and* the scope of what a person can do (p. 67)?
   a. Licensure
   b. Registration
   c. Certification
   d. Licensure and Certification
   e. Registration and Certification
   f. Registration and Licensure
   g. All of the above

21. Which of the following is true (p. 67)?
   a. Licensed psychologists can prescribe medications for emotional problems only
   b. School psychologists can get licensed as clinical psychologists by taking the national psychology exam
   c. Many states now offer hospital privileges for licensed psychologists
   d. The American Psychological Association (APA) licenses psychologists.

22. Credentialing for marriage and family therapists has occurred as a result of the efforts of which of the following (p. 68)?
  a. AAMFT c. State counseling associations
  b. IAMFC **d.** All of the above

23. Certification for psychiatrists is controlled by which of the following (p.68)?
  a. The American Psychiatric Association
  b. The American Board of Psychiatry
  c. State licensing boards
  d. American Board of Neurology and Psychiatry

24. NBCC certifies counselors in all but which of the following areas (pp. 68-69)?
  a. School counseling
  b. Clinical mental health counseling
  c. Approved clinical supervisor
  d. Addictions counseling become certified
  e. Two of the above
  f. Three of the above
  g. None of the above (all can through NBCC)

25. According to Neukrug, Milliken, & Walden (2001), approximately how many counselors are today credentialed throughout the country (p. 69)?
  a. 10,000 c. 50,000 e. 100,00
  b. 85,000 **d.** 140,000

26. Which of the following is true about counselor lobbying efforts (pp. 69-70)? (www)
  a. All counselors must become active in lobbying efforts if we are to meet our goals.
  b. Many counseling associations now hire professional lobbyists
  c. A proportion of our professional fees usually go to lobbying efforts
  d. All of the above
  e. None of the above

27. Relative to multicultural issues, which is true about the ACA ethical guidelines (p. 70)?
  a. It addresses multicultural issues in a multitude of ways
  b. Some say it does not go far enough in addressing multicultural issues
  c. Among other things, they state that counselors must show that they have taken course work or continuing education credits in multicultural counseling
  d. a and b
  e. b. and c
  f. a and c
  g. All of the above

28. The multicultural competencies developed by AMCD (p. 71): (www)
  a. are mandatory
  b. address the beliefs, knowledge, and skills counselors trainees should learn
  c. address issues of counselor awareness, understanding of the world view of the client, and interventions that should be used with culturally different clients.
  d. Two of the above
  e. All of the above

29. Professionalism in a profession is marked by all but which of the following (p. 72)?
  a. Becoming credentialied
  b. Attending conferences and continuing education workshops
  c. Obtaining supervision
  d. Abiding by ethical guidelines when reasonable
  e. Embodying "professional" personal characteristics
  f. Being a mentor to others
  g. Joining professional associations
  h. None of the above (all are marks of professionalism)

True or False

33. CACREP requires that all accredited counseling programs have a coursework in social and cultural issues (pp. 64-65) (**T**).

34. Today, all states have obtained licensing for counselors (p. 69) (**F**).

35. An individual who goes through a CACREP accredited program can take the National Counselor Exam prior to graduation (pp. 68-69) (**T**).

36. IAMFC offers a national certification process for marriage and family counseling (p. 68) (**T**).

37. Any licensed physician can call himself or herself a psychiatrist (p. 68) (**T**).

38. Today, licensure for clinical or counseling psychologists occurs only on the doctoral level (p. 67) (**T**).

39. In today's world, it can almost always be assumed that a person who is licensed has had more experience, course work, and supervision, than a person who is not (pp. 66-69) (**T**).

40. Approximately 70% of all counseling programs are now accredited (p. 64) (**F**).

41. If you work for an agency or at an educational setting, you are likely to be covered by an umbrella malpractice insurance policy (p. 62) (**T**).

42. It is wise to be covered by additional malpractice even if your agency or school has an umbrella malpractice insurance policy (p. 62) (**T**).

43. Generally, if one is not satisfied with the conclusion that may be found in a code of ethics, such as ACAs, one should seek a different explanation in a related professional code of ethics such as APAs (p. 58) (**F**).

44. Recently, there has been a push toward unifying all of the ethical guidelines of ACAs divisions into the main ethical code of ACA (p. 71) (**T**).

45. The use of ethical codes by counselors, psychologists, and social workers can be traced back to the origins of the professions in the 1800s (p. 51) (**F**).

46. What might be unethical behavior for one person, could be ethical for another (pp. 51-52) (**T**).

47. Generally, there is little disparity among counselors' perception of what is ethical (p. 53) (**F**).

48. Ethical guidelines are guidelines that assist the counselor in his or her ethical decision making; are moral not legal documents written by our professional associations based on a "consensus of morality," to which we are expected to abide(pp. 50-52) (**T**).

49. APA and NASW are slightly behind counselors in their ability to get licensure adapted by the 50 states (pp. 67-69) (**F**).

50. Anybody can sue anybody for anything (p. 62) (**T**).

51. Ethical codes are *not* easily enforced (p. 54) (**T**).

52. Ethical guidelines can be brought to court to show the court that the counselor acted in a responsible and professional manner (pp. 61-62) (**T**).

INFOTRAC KEY WORDS: Ethical decision making models. Credentialing. Accreditation. CACREP.

CHAPTER 4

THE HELPING RELATIONSHIP
INDIVIDUAL APPROACHES TO COUNSELING

Multiple Choice

1. A counseling theory offers us which of the following (p. 77)?
   a. A system of doing counseling
   b. Assistance in applying techniques
   c. Guidelines for predicting client change
   d. Two of the above
   e. All of the above

2. Eclecticism is which of the following (p. 78)? (www)
   a. The integration of aspects of various theories into one approach
   b. Always focused on one particular theory while integrating specific skills of other theories
   c. Not used by many counselors today
   d. Two of the above
   e. Three of the above

3. Psychodynamic theory proposes all but which of the following (p. 79)?
   a. Personality is constructed through a complex interaction of a person's drives with his or her early experiences
   b. An individual's behaviors are a result of early childhood patterning and are often unconscious
   c. Personality is fairly well determined by early patterns.
   d. Satisfaction of higher order needs can lead to changes in personality.

4. A theory's view of human nature takes into account the effects of _________, _________, and _________ on the personality development of an individual (p. 77).
   a. biology, sociology and morality
   b. biology, genetics and environment
   c. environment, ethnicity and ability
   d. None of the above

5. Which of the following is *not* considered a psychodynamic or a neo-Freudian theorist (p. 79)?
   a. Alfred Adler
   b. Carl Jung
   c. Harry Stack Sullivan
   d. Wilhelm Reich
   e. Otto Rank
   f. Melanie Klein
   g. Heinz Kohut
   h. Two of the above
   i. All are neo-Freudian or Psychodynamic arena

6. The psychoanalytic life instincts are (p. 80):
   a. sometimes called the libido
   b. the instinct toward destruction
   c. the instinct toward the continuation of the species
   d. a and c
   d. a and b

7. With which energy system does Freud suggest people are born (p. 80)?
   a. The superego **b.** The id c. The libido d. The ego

8. Which energy system is ruled by the reality principle (p. 80)? (www)
   A. The id **b.** The ego c. The superego d. B and C

9. In which psychosexual stage does the child develop a sense of control over the world (p. 81)?
   a. Phallic **b.** Anal c. Oral d. Latency e. Genital

10. In which psychosexual stage does little occur developmentally (p. 82)?
   a. Phallic b. Anal c. Oral **d.** Latency e. Genital

11. In the Phallic stage, which of the following occurs (p. 81)?
   a. The child develops a sense of trust and security in the world
   b. The child gains control over his or her bowels
   c. The child is particularly affected by the moral imperatives of parents
   d. None of the above

12. Replacing a perceived negative feeling with a positive one is the use of which defense mechanism (p. 82)?
   a. Regression   b. Identification   c. Compensation   d. Reaction formation

13. Transference is (pp. 82-83):
   a. saying whatever comes to mind without filtering
   b. resisting treatment
   c. projecting the characteristics of others onto the therapist
   d. the "royal road to the unconscious"

14. Dreams may be analyzed by examining both the__________, and the___________content of the dream (p. 83)
   a. latent; thanatos   c. manifest; thanatos
   b. latent; animus   d. latent; manifest

15. Psychoanalysis (p. 83):
   a. is an in-depth therapy
   b. stresses childhood experiences
   c. focuses on bringing the unconscious to the surface
   d. stresses that the counselor remain aloof from the client
   e. Two of the above
   f. All of the above

16. Which is the correct order of Freud's psychosexual stages of development (pp. 81-82)?
   a. Oral, anal, genital, phallic, latency
   b. Oral, anal, phallic, genital, latency
   c. Oral, anal, genital, latency, phallic
   d. Oral, anal, phallic, latency, genital

17. Irving receives erotic pleasure from having bowel movements. He is in which of Freud's stages (p. 81)?
   a. Genital   b. Phallic   c. Oral   d. Anal   e. Latency

18. Wayne hates to spend money, but he constantly criticizes his wife for being too "stingy." This represents the defense mechanism of (p. 82)?
   a. Projection   c. Rationalization   e. Identification
   b. Repression   d. Sublimation   f. Compensation

19. The act of pushing certain memories out of our consciousness because they create too much anxiety is known as which of the following (p. 82)?
   a. Repression.   c. Intellectualization   e. Identification
   b. Sublimation.   d. Projection.   f. Rationalization

20. Which represents Freud's "Structure of Personality?" (pp. 80-81)?
   a. Id, ego, superego
   b. Oral, anal, phallic, latency, genital stages
   c. Defense mechanisms
   d. All of the above

21. Sylvester enjoys playing with his own genitals. He is probably in which of Freud's stages? (p. 81).
   a. Genital   b. Phallic   c. Oral   d. Anal   e. Latency

22. According to Freud, this part of the personality represents the formation of morality and is influenced by the values of parents and society: (pp. 79-80)
   a. Ego **b.** Superego c. Id d. Libido

23. Jung's collective unconscious is (p. 84):
   a. a description of universal moral truths
   b. a depository of ancient experiences
   c. both positive and negative
   d. revealed through archetypes
   e. Two of the above
   f. Three of the above
   g. All of the above

24. Jung's concept of the personal unconscious is (p. 84): (www)
   a. unique to each individual
   b. capable of becoming conscious
   c. incapable of becoming conscious
   d. a and b
   e. a and c

25. The first step toward integration and self-acceptance in Jungian therapy is (p. 84):
   a. awareness of our persona
   b. awareness of our shadow
   c. awareness of one's animas and animus
   d. all of the above

26. The Persona is (p. 84):
   a. the mask we wear in public life
   b. the feminine and masculine characteristics we all have
   c. the darkest, most hidden, and scariest parts of ourselves
   d. an archetype
   e. Two of the above
   f. Three of the above
   g. All of the above

27. Relative to our unconscious, Jung did *not* believe which of the following (p. 84)?
   a. It is important to raise consciousness of all parts of ourselves
   b. Like Freud, our unconscious can be accessed through dreams and free association
   c. Symbols hold hidden meanings about ourselves
   d. The Shadow and other unconscious parts need to remain repressed if we are to live a healthy life.

28. Which of the following is *not* an archetype (p. 84)?
   a. The anima b. The animus c. The persona d. The Shadow **e.** The id

29. Which of the following best represents Adler's belief about early childhood experiences (pp. 84-85)?
   a. Our experiences determine later behaviors.
   b. Early childhood experiences have little or no affect on the change process.
   c. It's not what happened to us, it's the memory and interpretation of what happened to us.
   d. Our place in our family of origin affects personality development
   e. Two of the above
   f. Three of the above
   g. All of the above.

30. According to Adler, feelings of inferiority (p. 84):
   a. are motivating
   b. are based on our perceptions of the past
   c. can lead us toward completeness
   d. None of the above
   e. All of the above

31. Social interest is (p. 85):
   a. a sense of connectedness to others and a worldwide community
   b. an indication of one's ability to be extroverted
   c. an important technique used in Adlerian therapy
   d. of little importance in Adlerian therapy

32. Which of the following represents the correct order of Mahler's four stages of development (p. 85):
   a. Autism, symbiosis, separation/individuation, constancy
   b. Symbiosis, autism, separation/individuation, constancy
   c. Autism, constancy, symbiosis, separation/individuation
   d. Symbiosis, autism, constancy, separation/individuation

33. Splitting is (p. 85):
   a. a term used by Freud to describe the separation of the id, ego, and superego
   b. an important developmental process that allows the adult to see the world in dualistic ways
   c. an object-relations theory defense mechanism important for children, but potentially harmful for adults
   d. the result of the disintegration of archetypes

34. Which of the following is an object relations theorist (p. 85)?
   a. Freud
   b. Adler
   c. Jung
   d. Mahler
   e. a and b
   f. b and d

35. Existential-humanistic approaches believe all but which of the following (p. 86)?
   a. Early experiences pattern later development and determine personality structures
   b. There is an inborn tendency to self-actualize
   c. Consciousness is more important than unconsciousness
   d. Anxiety is a natural part of living and a message about one's existence
   e. The subjective worldview of the client is crucial in the therapeutic process
   f. Two of the above are incorrect

36. Philosophers such as Kierkegaard, Tillich, Sartre, and Camus are associated with which approach to counseling (p. 86)?
   a. Psychodynamic **b.** Existential-Humanistic c. Behavioral d. Cognitive

37. The founder of person-centered counseling is (pp. 86-87): (www)
   a. Fritz Perls b. Abraham Maslow c. Viktor Frankl **d.** Carl Rogers

38. The main goal of person-centered counseling is to (p. 87):
   a. have greater awareness of how one's past affects present day behavior
   b. to change the manner in which we feel about ourselves
   c. to find new behaviors that can replace old, maladaptive behaviors
   d. to become more in touch with one's "true self."

39. Person-centered counseling relies on which of the following counselor qualities (p. 87)?
   a. Realness, reflection of feelings, self-awareness
   b. Empathy, awareness of unconscious, advocacy
   c. Sympathy, identification, actualization
   d. Empathy, geneuineness, unconditional positive regard

40. The ability to hear feelings beyond what the client is saying is called (p. 89):
   a. basic empathy **b.** subceiving c. congruence d. awareness

41. Conditions of worth are (p. 89):
   a. positive qualities parents attempt to give to us
   b. secondary reinforcers, such as tokens.
   c. conditions placed on us by significant people in order to get us to act in a certain manner
   d. a positive way of understanding changes in the therapeutic relationship

42. In person-centered counseling, the therapeutic relationship is (p. 89):
   a. a key factor in counseling
   b. a negligent factor in counseling
   c. at times a small factor, while other times a major factor
   d. the result of therapist anonymity

43. Congruence is (p. 88):
   a. when the counselor is in touch with his or her feelings
   b. a core factor in the person-centered therapeutic relationship
   c. not as important as the use of interpretation
   d. Two of the above
   e. None of the above

44. A client is nervously wriggling during a session, at which point the counselor says, "You seem rather anxious today." The client responds, "No, I feel just fine." The counselor's response was which of the following (p. 89)?
   a. A higher-level empathic response as the counselor identified a feeling of which the client is not aware.
   b. An important confrontation in person-centered counselor
   c. A lower-level empathic response because the client denied the counselor's statement.
   d. None of the above

45. Perls' approach to counseling is which of the following (p. 90)?
   a. Existentially-humanistically based
   b. Confrontational
   c. Antideterministic
   d. Phenomenonlogically focused
   e. Two of the above
   f. Three of the above
   g. All of the above

46. Which of the following is *not* a term that is used in Gestalt Therapy (pp. 90-92)?
   a. The "now"
   b. Unfinished business
   c. Impasse
   d. External supports
   e. Implosion

47. Which of the following techniques is *not* used in Gestalt Therapy (pp. 91-92)?
   a. The exaggeration technique
   b. Flooding
   c. Empty chair technique
   d. Awareness Exercises
   e. Use of "I" statements
   f. Playing the projection

48. All but which of the following are well known existential therapists (p. 92)?
   a. Arbuckle b. May c. Frankl d. Mahoney e. All are

49. Which of the following is *not* a basic tenet of existential therapy (p. 92)?
   a. People have the capacity for self-awareness,
   b. People have the ability to make some choices
   c. We create our identity to establish meaningful relationships with others
   d. Part of the process of living naturally involves the search for meaning
   e. Understanding our ways of irrational living is crucial to recreating a new life course
   f. The nature of choice means that anxiety is a natural condition of living

50. Which of the following techniques is most associated with existential therapy (p. 92)?
   a. The use of interpretation
   b. The use of confrontation
   c. The use of questions
   d. Pointing out contradictions
   e. Existential theorists stress the relationship, not "techniques"

51. Which is *not* true about existential therapists (p. 92)? (www)
   a. They tend to be more didactic than person-centered therapists
   b. They tend not to be as confrontational as the gestalt therapist
   c. They tend to offer interpretive comments, much like psychodynamic therapists
   d. They usually feel free to use any techniques that will raise the consciousness of the client concerning the basic existential principles.

52. Based on the readings in the text, which of the following is *not* considered in the behavioral school (pp. 93-99)?
   a. Pavlov
   b. Skinner
   c. Watson
   d. Lazarus
   e. Wolpe
   f. Glasser
   g. Bandura
   h. Ellis

53. Which theorist(s) is(are) *incorrectly* associated with the following behavioral concepts? (p. 93)?
   a. Skinner--Classical Conditioning
   b. Pavlov--Operant Conditioning
   c. Bandura--Modeling
   d. a and b
   e. b and c
   f. All of the Above

54. Which of the following would be stressed by behaviorists (p. 93)?
   a. Unconsciousness
   b. The past
   c. Meaning-making
   d. Insight into experiences
   e. Problem identification

55. What is the correct order of the therapeutic stages in behaviorism (pp. 94-95)?
   a. Defining the Problem and setting goals, relationship building, choosing techniques, assessment, closure and follow-up
   a. Defining the problem and setting goals, relationship building, assessment, choosing techniques, closure and follow-up
   c. Relationship building, defining the problem and setting goals, choosing techniques, assessment, closure and follow-up
   d. Relationship building, choosing techniques, defining the problem and setting goals, assessment, closure and follow-up

56. A client with whom I am working has a fear of dirt. She remarks that her parents would always yell and scream at her when she was younger and playing in the dirt. In terms of behavioral principles, which approach most likely accounts for the client's fear (pp. 93, 95)?
   a. Modeling b. Classical conditioning c. Operant conditioning d. Flooding

57. In working with the client in the previous question, I decided to set up a hierarchy of fears and then I have her relax as I bring her through the hierarchy. This approach is called which of the following (pp. 95-96)?
   a. Self-management
   b. Flooding and implosion
   c. Modeling
   d. Systematic Desensitization
   e. Hierarchical approximations

58. I take a client who is afraid of elevators to the Empire State Building and ride up and down in elevators with him all day long. This approach is called which of the following (p. 96)? (www)
   a. Self-management
   b. Flooding and implosion
   c. Modeling
   d. Systematic Desensitization
   e. Hierarchical approximations

59. Reinforcing a child for *not* going into the street by saying, "Good job," and by offering M & Ms is the use of (p. 93).
   a. classical Conditioning
   b. modeling
   c. self-management
   d. multimodal
   e. operant conditioning

60. Which of the following is *not* important in the therapeutic relationship for the behavioral counselor (p. 96)?
   a. Rapport and trust
   b. Collaboration
   c. Problem identification
   d. Goal setting
   e. None of the above (all are important)

61. Multimodal therapy was developed by (p. 97):
   a. Watson b. Wolpe c. Bandura d. Skinner e. Lazarus

62. The BASIC ID is a(n) (pp. 97-98):
   a. description of one of Freud's structures of personality
   b. description of domains that should be looked at in multimodal therapy
   c. acronym for irrational thinking used by Ellis
   d. None of the above

63. Which of the following developed Reality Therapy (p. 98)?

a. Pavlov	c. Watson	e. Wolpe	g. Bandura
b. Skinner	d. Lazarus	f. Glasser	h. Ellis

64. Which of the following developed Choice Theory (p. 98)?

a. Pavlov	c. Watson	e. Wolpe	g. Bandura
b. Skinner	d. Lazarus	f. Glasser	h. Ellis

65. Behavior is the control of our perceptions (BCP) is a statement from a(n) (p. 98):
   a. operant conditioning therapist
   b. reality therapist
   c. gestalt therapist
   d. rational emotive therapist
   e. None of the above

66. According to Glasser, which of the following are inborn needs (p. 98)?
   a. belonging, power, freedom, fun, and survival
   b. safety, belonging, self-esteem, self-actualization
   c. hunger, thirst, sex, aggression
   d. All of the above

67. "You are depressing yourself," might be a statement made by (pp. 98-99):
   a. a person-centered counselor
   b. a gestalt therapist
   c. a behaviorist
   d. a reality therapist
   e. a constructivist

68. Which of the following is *not* associated with reality therapy (pp. 98-99)?
   a. Building a friendship with the client
   b. Applying operant and classical conditioning principles
   c. Focusing on doing
   d. Having the client make plans
   e. Having the client following through
   f. Making a commitment and not giving up on the client

69. The differences between traditional cognitive therapists and constructivists include all but which of the following (pp. 99-100)?
   a. Traditionalists believe humans are best helped by replacing irrational thoughts, constructivists believe the humans are complex, with thinking being one aspect of their being.
   b. Traditionalists examine illogical/irrational beliefs, constructivists view thinking as a metaphor about one's existence.
   c. Traditionalists believe in unconscious motivations, constructivists only look at consciousness.
   d. Traditionalists view counseling as a process of replacing illogical thinking with rational/logical thinking. Constructivists help individuals look at new ways of constructing meaning-making.

70. The five steps of rational emotive behavior therapy include all but which of the following (p. 100)?
   a. Convince the client that he or she thinks irrationally
   b. Show the client how he or she maintains irrational thinking
   c. Help the client understand how to challenge irrational thinking
   d. Tell the client what new behaviors to adopt. Follow this up by having the client use "self talk" to convince him or herself that these are better new behaviors.
   e. Help the client understand how he or she has internalized one or more generalized irrational beliefs
   f. Help the client work on developing a more rational way of thinking

71. The ABC and Ds of REBT stand for all but which of the following (p. 101)? (www)
   a. A = Activating event
   b. B = Behavior that is the result of the event
   c. C = Consequences of the event
   d. D = Disputing irrational beliefs

72. Which of the following would *not* be used by an REBT therapist (p. 102)?
   a. Cognitive homework
   b. Role-playing
   c. Shame-attacking exercises
   d. Imagery
   e. Behavioral techniques
   f. Emotive techniques
   g. Two of the above
   h. Three of the above
   i. None of the above (all are used)

73. Which of the following is important to the therapeutic relationship of the REBT counselor (pp. 102-103)?
   a. The necessary and sufficient conditions
   b. Exploring transference and countertransference issues
   c. Having the client understand how stories represent a metaphor of one's existence
   d. Having the client believe in the REBT philosophy, regardless of whether or not the client likes the counselor.

74. Which of the following is *not* correctly matched (p. 104)?
   a. Structures ➡➡Events
   b. Processes ➡➡ Structures
   c. Events ➡➡ Processes
   d. All of the above are correctly matched

75. Aaron Beck's approach to cognitive therapy differs from Ellis' in all of the following ways except (p. 103):
   a. Beck is more concerned about the relationship between the client and the counselor
   b. Beck believes that the term "irrational" is too loaded for clients to buy into
   c. Beck focuses more on story telling and metaphors, Ellis on how people think
   d. Beck looks more at cognitive structures, Ellis at irrational thinking

76. Beck states that cognitive distortions could lead to all but which of the following (p. 104)?
   a. Dualistic thinking b. Overgeneralization c. Personalization **d.** Identification

77. Schemas are (p. 104):
   a. automatic thoughts that are out of consciousness
   b. faulty thinking
   c. the floor plan that influences how each individual thinks
   d. None of the above

78. Cognitive events are (p. 104):
   a. automatic thoughts that are out of consciousness
   b. faulty thinking
   c. the floor plan that influences how each individual thinks
   d. None of the above

79. Which school of therapy does Mahoney fall into (p. 104)?
   a. Traditional cognitive
   b. Cognitive-behavioral
   c. Constructivist
   d. Behavioral

80. Constructivists believe in all but which of the following (pp. 104-105)?
   a. Human knowing is active, anticipatory, and constantly being constructed
   b. There is no certifiable eternal "reality "
   c. Irrational thinking is a product of external events
   d. Deep underlying schema are more difficult to change than surface structures
   e. There is a complex interaction between one's feelings, thoughts, and actions

81. What place do narratives play in constructivist therapy (p. 105)? (www)
   a. The counselor uses narratives to show the client different ways of viewing the world.
   b. Narratives are ways of understanding the ABCs of thinking
   c. They reveal meaning about the client's ways of knowing the world
   d. They reveal knowledge about the counselor's way of understanding the client

82. Which of the following is *not* used by a constructivist therapist (pp. 104-105)?
   a. Empathy
   b. Metaphor
   c. Hypnotherapy
   d. Traditional cognitive techniques
   e. All of the above are used

83. Eclectism or integrative approaches to counseling are (p. 106):
  a. a mish mosh of approaches all put together into one approach
  b. a way of combining two or more approaches in a systematic fashion
  c. a way of integrating a client who is dissociating
  d. None of the above

84. Neukrug suggests that there is a developmental process that occurs in the creation of an eclectic approach. Of the choices below, which represents the order of this process (p. 106)?
  a. Chaos, theoretical integration, coalescence, metatheory
  b. Chaos, theoretical integration, metatheory, coalescence
  c. Theoretical integration, chaos, metatheory, coalescence
  d. Chaos, coalescence, theoretical integration, metatheory
  e. Theoretical integration, chaos, coalescence, metatheory

85. The coalescence stage of eclectism is highlighted by which of the following (p. 106)?
  a. Adherence to one approach and beginning attempts to integrate other techniques
  b. Disorder, ambivalence, and moment-to-moment subjective judgements
  c. The pulling together of all theories into one, integrative approach
  d. The understanding that there may be one overarching theory that can explain all theories.

86. The difference between brief approaches to counseling and solution-focused approaches includes all but which of the following (pp. 107-109)?
  a. Brief therapy focuses on the problem, solution-focused therapy does not
  b. Solution-focused therapy is cognitive by its nature, brief therapy is almost exclusively behavioral
  c. Solution focused therapy asks the "miracle" question
  d. Solution-focused therapy focuses more on the future as compared to brief therapy

87. Which of the following theoretical approaches tends to have little, if any, cross-cultural bias (pp. 109-110)?
  a. Psychoanalytic
  b. Existential-humanistic
  c. Behavioral
  d. Cognitive
  e. Brief-treatment approaches
  f. None of the above (all are biased)

88. The Tarassoff case did which of the following (p. 111)?
  a. It highlighted the negative consequences of dual relationships
  b. It stressed the importance of duty to warn
  c. It showed how information must be kept confidential
  d. It highlighted the importance of informed consent in the counseling relationship

89. Which of the following is the *primary* responsibility of counselors (p. 110)? (www)
  a. Assuring confidentiality
  b. Respecting diversity
  c. Avoiding harm
  d. Respecting the welfare of the client
  e. All of the above

True or False

90. The purpose of the miracle question in solution-focused therapy is to help the client highlight the problem so he or she can get down to working on the problem (pp. 108-109) (**F**).

91. The fastest growing approach to counseling these days is probably brief and solution-focused therapies (p. 107) (**T**).

92. Integrative approaches to counseling are sometimes called eclectism (pp. 105-106) (**T**).

93. Beck believes that by understanding certain types of structures, processes, and events lend themselves toward specific diagnostic categories (p. 104) (**T**).

94. Traditional cognitive therapists tend to use a dialectical process in helping the client create new cognitive structures (pp. 99-100) (**T**).

95. The use of emotive techniques is an important part of REBT (pp. 101-102) (**T**).

96. One of the most important skills an REBT counselor should use is empathy (pp. 102-103) (**F**).

97. Glasser believes that mental illness and most problems in life are created by the person (p. 98) (**T**).

98. Reality therapy is strongly antideterministic (p. 98) (**T**).

99. Lazarus' approach to counseling is straightforward and pragmatic (p. 98) (**T**).

100. Today, the relationship plays much less of a role in behavioral counseling than it use to (p. 96) (**F**).

101. Behavioral approaches stress unconscious thoughts (p. 93) (**F**).

102. A therapist who would encourage a client to turn questions into statements about self is probably coming from a Cognitive perpsective (p. 91) (**F**).

103. Existential therapists view therapy as a shared journey between an expert and a person who needs guidance and direction (p. 92) (**F**).

104. Unconditional positive regard implies that the therapist is approving of everything the client does (pp. 88-89) (**F**).

105. Roger's preferred to use the term "reflection of feelings" to describe his process of therapy (p. 89) (**F**).

106. The term congruence is interchangeable with the term genuineness (p. 88). (**T**).

107. Rogers believed that the individual's need to be regarded by others is so strong, that a person will act in a nongenuine way in order to obtain this regard (p. 87) (**T**).

108. The necessary and sufficient conditions for therapy to work include the ability to build an alliance, understanding the client's world from a systemic perspective, and quietly challenging the client to change (p. 88) (**F**).

109. Increased internal locus of control, increased congruence, more acceptance of others, increased openness to experience, better problem solving, and increased self regard are usually associated with the goals of object-relations theory (p. 86) (**F**).

110. Privileged communication is the legal right to refuse to cooperate with a legal request for information (usually a subpoena) about confidential disclosures (pp. 111-112) (**T**).

111. Like Freud, Mahler believed in the importance of the first few years of life affecting personality development (p. 85) (**T**).

112. Some believe Adler to be the first humanistic therapist (p. 85) (**T**).

113. Faulty assumptions are based on perceptions of our past and lead to our lifestyle (p. 84) (**T**).

114. Adler's concept of feelings of superiority, by its very nature, generally leads to narcissistic, self-aggrandizing behaviors (pp. 84-85) (**F**).

115. Adler believed that we are determined by our early experiences (p. 84) (**F**).

116. Jung believed that Freud's theory was too focused on psychopathology (pp. 83-84) (**T**).

117. In Freud's theory, the psychosexual stages affect the development of the structures of personality. (**T**) (p. 81)

118. According to Freud, the child is born with an id, but *not* with an ego or superego. (**T**) (p. 80)

119. Freud created the first comprehensive theory of psychotherapy (p. 77) (**T**).

120. Since a theory is heuristic, it is difficult to discard its ineffective aspects (p. 77) (**F**).

121. Psychodynamic theories are based primarily on conscious thought (p. 79) (**F**).
122. Psychoanalysis rarely lasts longer than 2 years (p. 83) (**F**).

123. The collective unconscious is revealed through archetypes (p. 84) (**T**).

124. Having a counseling relationship with a friend is always unethical (p. 111) (**T**).

125. In the spaces below, fill in the word that corresponds to the letter for Lazarus' BASIC ID (pp. 97-98).
B_______ A_______ S_______ I_______ C_______ I_______ D_______

(Questions 126-134) Fill in the Blanks

Match the correct defense mechanism, with the corresponding statement (p. 82).

a. Repression	d. Compensation	g. Sublimation
b. Rationalization	e. Regression	h. Identification
c. Denial	f. Projection	i. Reaction formation

126. _____ the distortion of reality in order to deny perceived threats to the person (**c**)
127. _____ the explaining away of a bruised or hurt ego (**b**)
128. _____ the pushing out of awareness of threatening or painful memories (**a**)
129. _____ reverting to an earlier stage of development with less demanding ways of responding to anxiety (**e**)
130. _____ viewing others as having unacceptable qualities that the individual himself or herself actually has (**f**)
131. _____ exaggerating certain positive traits in an effort to mask weaker traits (**d**)
132. _____ replacing a perceived negative feeling with a positive one (**i**)
133. _____ identifying with groups or others to improve one's sense of self-worth (**h**)
134. _____ channeling impulses into socially accepted forms of behavior (**g**)

INFOTRAC KEY WORDS: Psychodynamic. Existential therapy. Behavioral therapy. Cognitive therapy. Brief Treatment. Eclecticism. Integrative therapy.

CHAPTER 5

COUNSELING SKILLS

Multiple Choice

1. The counseling environment includes all but which of the following (p. 115)?
   a. The office
   b. Nonverbal behavior and touch
   c. Counselor qualities to embrace
   d. Counselor qualities to avoid
   e. Two of the above
   f. Al of the above

2. A counselor decides to place pro-choice literature in her office. This action is (pp. 115-116): (www)
   a. illegal
   b. unethical
   c. illegal and unethical
   d. neither illegal nor unethical, but may turn off some clients

3. Having physical contact with a client should be based on all but which of the following (p. 116)?
   a. The counselor's assessment of the client's ability to handle touch
   b. The counselor's awareness of his or her own needs
   c. Whether or not touch would be helpful to the counseling relationship
   d. An analysis of what is ethical, legal, and what has been practiced in the setting
   e. None of the above (all are important)

4. Relative to cross-cultural issues, which is *not* correct (pp. 116-117)?
   a. Some cultures are more comfortable with eye contact than others
   b. Some cultures will be offended by certain types of touch
   c. Some cultures would be offended by a counselor leaning forward
   d. Nonverbal language is universal, regardless of culture
   e. None of the above are incorrect

5. Of the following attitudes and behaviors, which should a counselor *not* try to avoid (p. 117)?
   a. Being critical of the client
   b. Being disbelieving of the client
   c. Scolding the client
   d. Punishing the client
   e. Disapproving of the client
   f. Threatening the client
   g. Rejecting the client
   h. None of the above (all should be avoided)

6. Which of the following is *not* considered an essential skill (pp. 117-121)?
   a. Self-esteem building and affirmations
   b. Listening skills
   c. Empathy
   d. Silence
   e. None of the above (all are essential)

7. Which of the following is usually *not* a hindrance to listening (p. 119)?
   a. Asking questions
   b. Distractions
   c. Having a strong emotional reaction to your client's concerns
   d. Thinking about what you're going to say
   e. Having preconceived notions about what the client is going to say
   f. None of the above, all can be hindrances to listening

8. Empathy is (p. 119):
   a. the ability to identify with the client
   b. the projection of the client's experiences onto the counselor
   c. the ability to sympathize with the client
   d. the ability to perceive the internal frame of reference of the client
   e. Two of the above

9. Who developed a scale to measure the ability to make empathic responses (pp. 119-120)? (www)
   a. Truax b. Carkhuff c. Rogers **d.** a and b e. b and c f. All of the above

10. Who was most credited for the popularity of the use of empathy in counseling (p. 119)?
   a. Truax b. Carkhuff **c.** Rogers d. a and b e. b and c f. All of the above

11. On the Carkhuff scale a "level 3" response (p. 120):
   a. accurately reflects affect and meaning of the client's statement
   b. subtracts from the affect and/or meaning of the client's statement
   c. adds to the affect and/or meaning of the client's statement
   d. None of the above

12. On the Carkhuff scale, a response above a "level 3" (pp. 120-121):
   a. accurately reflects affect and meaning of the client's statement
   b. subtracts from the affect and/or meaning of the client's statement
   c. adds to the affect and/or meaning of the client's statement
   d. None of the above

13. In response to a client's statement that he feels stuck, a counselor says, "Sounds like you're mired in the mud." This type of response is (p. 121):
   a. an example of the use of metaphor d. a and b
   b. a low-level response e. b and c
   c. a high-level response **f.** a and c

14. Questions can be helpful in all of the following ways, except (p. 122):
   a. They help the client have a sense that he or she is leading the direction of the counseling relationship
   b. The help uncover historical patterns
   c. They help find underlying issues
   d. The can gently challenge the client to change

15. As compared to closed questions, open questions (p. 123):
   a. provide greater client options when making responses
   b. should rarely be used
   c. are considered worse than closed questions
   d. None of the above

16. Which of the following is true about questions (pp. 123-124)?
   a. They can lead to an authoritarian helping relationship
   b. They can make the client feel humiliated and dependent
   c. Generally, the are not as facilitative as empathic responses
   d. They can be helpful in uncovering patterns and gently challenging clients to change
   e. Two of the above
   f. All of the above

17. A counselor asks her client, "Were you happy or sad in your marriage?" This is an example of a (p. 123)?
   a. Closed question c. Strategic question
   b. Open Question d. Reflective Question

18. The example given in question 17 is (p. 123):
   a. generally considered a good questioning technique
   b. generally considered a poor questioning technique
   c. neither poor, nor good. It depends on the situation
   d. an example of a question that should never be used

18. Indirect questions are often very similar to (p. 123): (www)
   a. lineal questioning c. open questions
   b. circular questioning **d.** empathic responding

20. Why questions (p. 123):
   a. should generally be avoided
   b. should be used often
   c. should never be used
   d. would be very helpful if the client could truly answer honestly
   e. a and b
   f. b and c
   g. b and c

21. Self disclosure (pp. 124-125):
   a. Should generally be avoided
   b. Can foster deeper intimacy in the counseling relationship
   c. Should never be used
   d. Should be used often
   e. a and b
   f. b and d

22. Content self-disclosure is when ______ , process self-disclosure is when ______ (p. 124).
   a. a counselor reveals information about self; a client reveals how he or she feels about the counselor in the moment
   b. a client reveals information about self; a counselor reveals how he or she feels about the client in the moment
   c. a client reveals information about self; a client reveals how he or she feels about the counselor in the moment
   d. a counselor reveals information about self; a counselor reveals how he or she feels about the client in the moment

23. A counselor decides to show his client how to act in an assertive manner at a restaurant. She therefore role-plays a situation for the client in which she plays a person who is *not* getting served. This is an example of which of the following (p. 126)?
   a. Circuitous modeling
   b. Linear modeling
   c. Strategic modeling
   d. Direct modeling
   e. Intentional modeling
   f. Reflective modeling

24. A client tells his counselor that he was very successful in listening to his wife because he modeled what the counselor had done with him during their sessions. This is called (p. 126):
   a. circuitous modeling
   b. linear modeling
   c. strategic modeling
   d. direct modeling
   e. intentional modeling
   f. reflective modeling

25. Which of the following is a foundational counseling skill (pp. 117-125)?
   a. Modeling
   b. Asking questions
   c. Empathy
   d. Self-disclosure
   e. Two of the above
   f. Three of the above
   g. All of the above

26. The best type of confrontation is which of the following (pp. 126-127)?
   a. Hard, fast, and to the point
   b. Used at the beginning of a relationship
   c. Used only after trust and rapport have been established
   d. Seen as a slight challenge to the client's way of viewing the world
   e. Two of the above Black Board
   f. Three of the above
   g. All of the above

27. Confrontation often involves the pointing out of discrepancies to the client. Which of the following is *not* a client discrepancy (p. 127)?
   a. Discrepancies between a client's feelings and behaviors
   b. Discrepancies between a client's values and behaviors
   c. Discrepancies between a client's verbal statements about self
   d. Discrepancies between a client's verbal expression of feelings and underlying feelings
   e. None of the above, all are potential discrepancies to point out to a client

28. Which of the following is *not* used to point out discrepancies in clients (pp. 127-128)?
    a. You/but statements
    b. Asking the client to justify the discrepancy
    c. Reframing
    d. Using Satire
    e. Higher-level empathy
    f. Two of the above
    g. None of the above (all are used to point out discrepancies)

29. A client tells a counselor how lazy his son is. A few weeks later, in reference to the client's son, who has been sitting around all day doing nothing, the counselor says, "You son really thinks carefully about what he wants to do before doing it." This is an example of which of the following (p. 128)?
    a. Confrontation
    b. Use of satire
    c. Two of the above
    d. Higher-level empathy
    e. Reframing
    f. None of the above

30. Which of the following is *not* true of interpretation (pp. 128-129)?
    a. It should never be used
    b. It can assist the client in making major therapeutic leaps in counseling
    c. It can set up the counselor as "the expert" and thus develop a dependent relationship
    d. Has not been shown to be strongly related to client outcomes
    e. Two of the above are not true

31. Which of the following skills is *not* listed in the text as a commonly used advanced skill (pp. 126-128)?
    a. Modeling
    b. Interpretation
    c. Confrontation
    d. All of the above are commonly used advanced skills

32. A major problem with the use of encouragement, affirmation, and self-esteem building includes which of the following (p. 130)? (www)
    a. Their use may foster a therapeutic relationship based on external validation
    b. They are too contrived
    c. They are difficult responses to formulate
    d. All of the above

33. Of "offering alternatives," "information giving," and "advice giving," the response that has the most potential for harm is __________ and the one that has the least potential for harm is __________ (p. 130).
    a. Offering alternatives; information giving
    b. Offering alternatives; advice giving
    c. Information giving; advice giving
    d. Advice giving; offering alternatives
    e. Advice giving; information giving
    f. All of the above are equally harmful

34. Which of the following represents the correct order of the stages of the counseling relationship (pp. 133-136)?
    a. Rapport and trust building, problem identification, deepening understanding and goal setting, work, closure, revolving door
    b. Rapport and trust building, deepening understanding and goal setting, problem identification, work, closure, revolving door
    c. Problem identification, rapport and trust building, deepening understanding and goal setting, work, closure, revolving door
    d. Problem identification, rapport and trust building, work, deepening understanding and goal setting, closure, revolving door

35. Case conceptualization (p. 131):
   a. should rarely be used by beginning counselors
   b. is rarely used by experienced counselors
   c. is a method to understand presenting problems and subsequently apply appropriate counseling skills
   d. is a type of counseling skill

36. The inverted pyramid model of case conceptualization does all but which of the following (p. 132)?
   a. Helps identify symptomatic behavior
   b. Helps place client difficulties into logical groupings
   c. Suggests specific theoretical orientations to use with clients who are experiencing certain problems
   d. Ties symptoms to deeper theoretical, interpretive, or causal references
   e. Helps to narrow symptoms to the client's most basic difficulties based and matches those difficulties to a number of theoretical orientations

37. Which can be detrimental to termination of the counseling relationship (p. 136)? (www)
   a. Discussing termination early
   b. Having clear goals
   c. Discussing feelings about termination
   d. Discussing the successes of the counseling relationship
   e. Discussing the fact that clients can return to counseling at a future date
   f. Opening up new issues near the end of the relationship

38. Near the end of the counseling relationship a client begins to miss sessions, ask for more time during sessions, becomes angry at the counselor, and brings up new issues. Most likely the client is (p. 136):
   a. needing to not terminate counseling
   b. needing to delve more deeply into a particular issue that has not been focused upon
   c. exhibiting anxiety about termination
   d. telling the counselor that counseling has not been successful for him or her
   e. Two of the above

39. Records can be shared with others in all but which of the following instances (pp. 138)?
   a. When information is shared with a supervisor
   b. If parents request information about their children
   c. If your client gives permission in writing to share information
   d. If the court subpoenas your records and you do not have privileged communication
   e. None of the above (records must be shared in all of the above situations)

40. Which of the following laws or court decisions assures that parents have access to their children's educational records (p. 140)? (www)
   a. The Freedom of Information Act
   b. The Buckley Amendment
   c. Jaffee v. Redmond
   d. Donaldson v. O'Connor

41. Which of the following laws or court decisions will likely protect all licensed therapists from revealing client information in federal courts and possibly in all courts (p. 140)?
   a. The Freedom of Information Act
   b. The Buckley Amendment
   c. Jaffee v. Redmond
   d. Donaldson v. O'Connor

42. Privileged communication means that (pp. 140-141):
   a. all counselors have the right to confidentiality
   b. all counselors have the right to confidentiality in courts
   c. the legal right to not reveal confidential client information
   d. the ethical right to not reveal confidential client information.

True or False

43. Some say that as much as 80% of the meaning of messages is derived from nonverbal language (p. 116) **(T)**.

44. It is unethical to hug your client, except if there is a special circumstance, such as the death of a client's family member (p. 116) **(F)**.

45. Good counselor nonverbals always include leaning forward, having good eye contact, and using touch sparingly (pp. 116-117) **(F)**.

46. Generally, counselor trainees should try to make additive responses when first using the Carkhuff scale (p. 120) **(F)**.

47. "Pause time" from culture to culture is fairly similar (p. 122) **(F)**.

48. Generally, if it feels good to self-disclose, the counselor should listen to his or her feelings and do so (p. 125) **(F)**.

49. Irony should never be used as a counseling skills (p. 128) **(F)**.

50. Advice giving should never be used as a counseling skill (p. 130) **(F)**.

51. Interpretation is based on one's intuitive sense of the client's predicament (pp. 128-130) **(F)**.

52. Generally, the use of advanced and specialized counseling skills often takes training beyond the master's degree (p. 131) **(T)**.

53. There is a direct relationship between the stages of the counseling relationship and the case conceptualization process (pp. 136-137) **(T)**.

54. There is a deepening reciprocal relationship among the skills that we use, our case conceptualization model, our theoretical orientation, and the stages of the counseling relationship (p. 137) **(T)**.

55. Counselors should never take case notes *during* the counseling relationship (p. 138) **(F)**.

56. Clients have an ethical and legal right to have information about them kept confidential (p. 138) **(T)**.

57. Clerical help should never have access to case records (p. 139) **(F)**.

58. Counseling skills learned in graduate school are cross-culturally effective (pp. 139-140) **(F)**.

59. Confidentiality is a legal right, privileged communication an ethical right (pp. 140-141) **(F)**.

60. Parents have the right to the records of their children (p. 140) **(T)**

INFOTRAC KEY WORDS: Jaffee. Privileged communication. Confidentiality. Counseling techniques.

CHAPTER 6

FAMILY COUNSELING

Multiple Choice

1. The theory that describes the functioning of all types of systems is called (p. 148):
   a. family systems theory
   b. general systems theory
   c. pluralistic theory
   d. the humanistic approach

2. Which of the following is an association for family counseling (p. 147)? (www)
   a. AAMFT
   b. IAMFC
   c. NASW
   d. APA
   e. Two of these
   f. Three of these

3. Which of the following is *not* true of the research on marital and family counseling (p. 148)?
   a. Family counseling is particularly good for some specific disorders
   b. Short-term family counseling seems as good as long-term treatment
   c. One school of family counseling is not necessarily better than another
   d. Ten percent of clients will get worse in family counseling
   e. None of the above (all are true)

4. Which of the following developed general systems theory (p. 148)?
   a. Minuchin
   b. Bertalanffy
   c. Bowen
   d. Satir
   e. Boszormenyi-nagy
   f. Haley

5. A couple begins to argue, and each time one individual says something, the other ups the ante to the point when the couple begin to hit one another. This is an example of which of the following (p. 150)?
   a. Homeostasis
   b. Scapegoating
   c. A positive feedback loop
   d. A negative feedback loop
   e. Two of the above
   f. None of the above

6. A healthy system has which of the following (p. 149)?
   a. Rigid boundaries
   b. Semipermeable boundaries
   c. Loose boundaries
   d. Highly developed boundaries

7. The tendency for components in a system to maintain their typical ways of functioning, whether those actions within the system are functional or dysfunctional, is called (p. 150): (www)
   a. equilibrium
   b. a competing tendency
   c. a conflicting tendency
   d. homeostasis

8. The death of a child or sibling would be an example of a (p. 154):
   a. situational crisis
   b. developmental cycle
   c. semi-idealistic crisis
   d. All of the above

9. In the example above, if the family has healthy ways of communicating, and if the family is able to support one another, the family will (pp. 154-155):
   a. not experience pain
   b. survive in a healthy manner
   c. not talk about their pain
   d. survive but with a great amount of dysfunction due to the severity of the crises

10. Which of the following is true of a scapegoat within a family system (p. 152)?
    a. He or she is usually an identified patient
    b. He or she takes the focus away from the real problem
    c. He or she provides a healthy way of the family to deal with problems
    d. Both a and b
    e. All of the above

11. Nearly what percent of marriages end in divorce (p. 151)?
 a. 33% b. 75% c. 50% d. Cannot be determined

12. The more serious the unfinished business from the past that husbands and wives bring into the marriage, the more likely it will (p. 152):
 a. not affect the marriage
 b. not affect the family
 c. affect both the family and the marriage
 d. not affect the family or the marriage

13. Healthy family systems have all but which of the following (p. 151)?
 a. Semipermeable boundaries
 b. Parents or guardians as the main "rule-makers"
 c. A clear sense of hierarchy
 d. Positive feedback loops
 e. None of the above (healthy systems have all of the above)

14. Regardless of the model of family employed, family counselors tend to apply skills based on all but which of the following (pp. 152-153)?
 a. Boundaries
 b. Homeostasis and feedback loops
 c. Equifinality
 d. Linear causality
 e. Subsystems and suprasystems

15. The school of family therapy most associated with Salvadore Minuchin is called which of the following (p. 153)?
 a. Psychodynamic
 b. Strategic
 c. Structural
 d. Experiential
 e. Multigenerational
 f. Communication
 g. Behavioral

16. Which of the following is *not* an important tenet of structural family therapy (p. 153-155)?
 a. Analysis of the undifferentiated ego mass
 b. Idiosyncratic and universal rules
 c. Analysis of systems and subsystems
 d. Mapping families
 e. Stress in families

17. Which of the following is *not* a type of stress as espoused by Minuchin (p. 154)?
 a. Extrafamilial
 b. Transitional
 c. Developmental
 d. Systemic
 e. Idiosyncratic

18. A mother is depressed and disengaged from her family and the father is stressed and overly involved with the three children. Which of the following would be an example of what a structural family therapist might do with this family (pp.:153-155)?
 a. Suggest to the father that he spend more time with his children so he can really show what a good parent he is, and suggest to mom that she find a hobby and spend less time with the family to allow dad to build the relationship because she's really not involved with the family anyway.
 b. Suggest to the parents that they find more "date time" together and that the grandmother become more involved in periodic parenting of the children.
 c. Tell dad how he seems like the mommy in the family and let mom know that you think she must either be missing the family or having an affair. Get them to express their feelings about your response. Act crazy with them.
 d. Review how the parent's early childhood experiences have patterned their current relationship styles.
 e. Help the family members get in touch with their feelings, be caring with them, and assist them in examining new ways of talking with one another.
 f. Examine how the "ghosts" of families from the past (e.g., grandparents, great-grandparents) continue to affect the manner in which the current family relates.
 g. Obtain a baseline of the kinds of activities that take place in the family and then develop goals and design strategies that will help the family meet the goals. Reinforce the new ways of relating in the family.

19. The school of family therapy most associated with Jay Haley is which of the following (p. 155)?
   a. Psychodynamic
   b. Strategic
   c. Behavioral
   d. Structural
   e. Experiential
   f. Multigenerational
   g. Communication

20. Which of the following represents the correct order of Haley's stages of the first interview (pp. 157-158)?
   a. Goal-setting stage, interaction stage, social stage, problem stage
   b. Interaction stage, goal-setting stage, social stage, problem stage
   c. Social stage, interaction stage, goal-setting stage, problem stage
   d. Social stage, problem stage, interaction stage, goal-setting stage

21. Strategic family therapy would stress all but which of the following (pp. 156-157)? (www)
   a. Normality is a contextual phenomenon
   b. Unconscious factors are important in understanding communication among people.
   c. Understanding communication is crucial to making changes in families
   d. An intervention made in a family, with one or more members, will reverberate throughout the family
   e. Understanding power tactics in families is important to making change in families

22. Telling a person what to do when the therapist does not want them to do it is an example of (pp. 158-159):
   a. poor family counseling
   b. helping the family understand their indebtedness and entitlements
   c. a paradoxical directive
   d. communication theory in practice

23. A mother is depressed and disengaged from her family and the father is stressed and overly involved with the three children. Which of the following would be an example of what a strategic family therapist might do with this family (pp.: 155-159)?
   a. Suggest to the father that he spend more time with his children so he can really show what a good parent he is, and suggest to mom that she find a hobby and spend less time with the family to allow dad to build the relationship because she's really not involved with the family anyway.
   b. Suggest to the parents that they find more "date time" together and that the grandmother become more involved in periodic parenting of the children.
   c. Tell dad how he seems like the mommy in the family and let mom know that you think she must either be missing the family or having an affair. Get them to express their feelings about your response. Act crazy with them.
   d. Review how the parent's early childhood experiences have patterned their current relationship styles.
   e. Help the family members get in touch with their feelings, be caring with them, and assist them in examining new ways of talking with one another.
   f. Examine how the "ghosts" of families from the past (e.g., grandparents, great-grandparents) continue to affect the manner in which the current family relates.
   g. Obtain a baseline of the kinds of activities that take place in the family and then develop goals and design strategies that will help the family meet the goals. Reinforce the new ways of relating in the family.

24. The school of family therapy most associated with Virginia Satir is called which of the following (p. 159)?
   a. Psychodynamic
   b. Strategic
   c. Behavioral
   d. Structural
   e. Experiential
   f. Multigenerational
   g. Communication

25. The primary survival triad includes (p. 160):
   a. the family counselor, parents, and children
   b. grandparents, parents, and children
   c. parents and the children
   d. All of the above

26. Which of the following is *not* an example of a communication pattern as described by Satir (p. 160)?

a. The manipulator
b. The placater
c. The computer
d. The distracter
e. The blamer

27. Which of the following is *not* stressed by Virginia Satir's approach to family counseling (pp. 160-161)?

a. Being in touch with one's feelings
b. Being clear on communication patterns
c. The importance of understanding multigenerational patterns
d. Having a strong sense of self
e. Seeing that differences are an opportunity to learn

28. A mother is depressed and disengaged from her family and the father is stressed and overly involved with the three children. Which of the following would be an example of what a communication family therapist might do with this family (pp.: 159-161)?

a. Suggest to the father that he spend more time with his children so he can really show what a good parent he is, and suggest to mom that she find a hobby and spend less time with the family to allow dad to build the relationship because she's really not involved with the family anyway.
b. Suggest to the parents that they find more "date time" together and that the grandmother become more involved in periodic parenting of the children.
c. Tell dad how he seems like the mommy in the family and let mom know that you think she must either be missing the family or having an affair. Get them to express their feelings about your response. Act crazy with them.
d. Review how the parent's early childhood experiences have patterned their current relationship styles.
e. Help the family members get in touch with their feelings, be caring with them, and assist them in examining new ways of talking with one another.
f. Examine how the "ghosts" of families from the past (e.g., grandparents, great-grandparents) continue to affect the manner in which the current family relates.
g. Obtain a baseline of the kinds of activities that take place in the family and then develop goals and design strategies that will help the family meet the goals. Reinforce the new ways of relating in the family.

29. The school of family therapy most associated with Boszormenyi-Nagy is which of the following (p. 161)?

a. Psychodynamic
b. Strategic
c. Behavioral
d. Structural
e. Experiential
f. Multigenerational
g. Communication

30. A ledger of indebtedness and entitlements is (p. 161):

a. passed down from past generations
b. attempted to be balanced by spouses
c. almost always unsuccessfully balanced by spouses
d. Two of the above
e. All of the above

31. The school of family therapy most associated with Murray Bowen is which of the following (p. 161)?

a. Psychodynamic
b. Strategic
c. Behavioral
d. Structural
e. Experiential
f. Multigenerational
g. Communication

32. Which of the following is *not* stressed by Bowen's family therapy approach (pp. 161-162)?

a. Understanding the family's undifferentiated ego mass
b. The use of genogram in understanding the family
c. The separation of the intellectual from emotional processes
d. The importance of understanding power dynamics in families

33. A mother is depressed and disengaged from her family and the father is stressed and overly involved with the three children. Which of the following would be an example of what a multigenerational family therapist might do with this family (pp.: 161-163)?
   a. Suggest to the father that he spend more time with his children so he can really show what a good parent he is, and suggest to mom that she find a hobby and spend less time with the family to allow dad to build the relationship because she's really not involved with the family anyway.
   b. Suggest to the parents that they find more "date time" together and that the grandmother become more involved in periodic parenting of the children.
   c. Tell dad how he seems like the mommy in the family and let mom know that you think she must either be missing the family or having an affair. Get them to express their feelings about your response. Act crazy with them.
   d. Review how the parent's early childhood experiences have patterned their current relationship styles.
   e. Help the family members get in touch with their feelings, be caring with them, and assist them in examining new ways of talking with one another.
   f. Examine how the "ghosts" of families from the past (e.g., grandparents, great-grandparents) continue to affect the manner in which the current family relates.
   g. Obtain a baseline of the kinds of activities that take place in the family and then develop goals and design strategies that will help the family meet the goals. Reinforce the new ways of relating in the family.

34. The school of family therapy most associated with Carl Whitaker is called which of the following (p. 163)? (www)
   a. Psychodynamic
   b. Strategic
   c. Behavioral
   d. Structural
   e. Experiential
   f. Multigenerational
   g. Communication

35. Which family therapist believed that therapy occurs in stages from defensiveness, to genuineness and openness, to discussion of inner conflicts, to facilitation by therapist, to members working on their own, to individuation and closure (p. 163)?
   a. Minuchin
   b. Whitaker
   c. Bowen
   d. Satir
   e. Boszormenyi-nagy
   f. Haley

36. A mother is depressed and disengaged from her family and the father is stressed and overly involved with the three children. Which of the following would be an example of what an experiential family therapist might do with this family (pp.: 163-164)?
   a. Suggest to the father that he spend more time with his children so he can really show what a good parent he is, and suggest to mom that she find a hobby and spend less time with the family to allow dad to build the relationship because she's really not involved with the family anyway.
   b. Suggest to the parents that they find more "date time" together and that the grandmother become more involved in periodic parenting of the children.
   c. Tell dad how he seems like the mommy in the family and let mom know that you think she must either be missing the family or having an affair. Get them to express their feelings about your response. Act crazy with them.
   d. Review how the parent's early childhood experiences have patterned their current relationship styles.
   e. Help the family members get in touch with their feelings, be caring with them, and assist them in examining new ways of talking with one another.
   f. Examine how the "ghosts" of families from the past (e.g., grandparents, great-grandparents) continue to affect the manner in which the current family relates.
   g. Obtain a baseline of the kinds of activities that take place in the family and then develop goals and design strategies that will help the family meet the goals. Reinforce the new ways of relating in the family.

37. The school of family therapy most associated with Nathan Ackerman and Robin Skynner is called which of the following (p. 164)?

a. Psychodynamic
b. Strategic
c. Behavioral
d. Structural
e. Experiential
f. Multigenerational
g. Communication

38. Which of the following is *not* true of psychodynamic family therapy (pp. 164-165)?

a. It attempts to combine concepts from psychodynamic theory and systemic thinking
b. It tends to be faster than individually oriented psychodynamic therapy
c. It stresses the importance of directives in order to speed up the process
d. Strategies and techniques vary for different psychodynamic therapists
e. Two of the above are not true

39. A mother is depressed and disengaged from her family and the father is stressed and overly involved with the three children. Which of the following would be an example of what a psychodynamic family therapist might do with this family (pp. 164-165)?

a. Suggest to the father that he spend more time with his children so he can really show what a good parent he is, and suggest to mom that she find a hobby and spend less time with the family to allow dad to build the relationship because she's really not involved with the family anyway.
b. Suggest to the parents that they find more "date time" together and that the grandmother become more involved in periodic parenting of the children.
c. Tell dad how he seems like the mommy in the family and let mom know that you think she must either be missing the family or having an affair. Get them to express their feelings about your response. Act crazy with them.
d. Review how the parent's early childhood experiences have patterned their current relationship styles.
e. Help the family members get in touch with their feelings, be caring with them, and assist them in examining new ways of talking with one another.
f. Examine how the "ghosts" of families from the past (e.g., grandparents, great-grandparents) continue to affect the manner in which the current family relates.
g. Obtain a baseline of the kinds of activities that take place in the family and then develop goals and design strategies that will help the family meet the goals. Reinforce the new ways of relating in the family.

40. The individual(s) most associated with behavioral family therapy is (p. 165):

a. Skinner b. Wolpe c. Lazarus d. Bandura e. None of the above

41. Which of the following behavioral approach is *not* used in behavioral family therapy (p. 156)? (www)

a. Operant conditioning
b. Classical conditioning
c. Modeling
d. Cognitive-behavioral approaches
e. Two of the above
f. None of the above (all are used in behavioral family therapy)

42. Which of the following is *not* a characteristic of behavioral family therapy (pp. 165-166)?

a. The importance of building a therapeutic relationship
b. Viewing therapy as time-limited and brief
c. Focusing on specific behaviors and using behavioral principles for the change process
d. Teaching clients the relationship among events from a behavioral perspective
e. Making sure that all family members are involved in the sessions
f. None of the above (all are characteristics)

43. A mother is depressed and disengaged from her family and the father is stressed and overly involved with the three children. Which of the following would be an example of what a behavioral family therapist might do with this family (pp. 165-166)?
   a. Suggest to the father that he spend more time with his children so he can really show what a good parent he is, and suggest to mom that she find a hobby and spend less time with the family to allow dad to build the relationship because she's really not involved with the family anyway.
   b. Suggest to the parents that they find more "date time" together and that the grandmother become more involved in periodic parenting of the children.
   c. Tell dad how he seems like the mommy in the family and let mom know that you think she must either be missing the family or having an affair. Get them to express their feelings about your response. Act crazy with them.
   d. Review how the parent's early childhood experiences have patterned their current relationship styles.
   e. Help the family member's get in touch with their feelings, be caring with them, and assist them in examining new ways of talking with one another.
   f. Examine how the "ghosts" of families from the past (e.g., grandparents, great-grandparents) continue to affect the manner in which the current family relates.
   <u>g.</u> Obtain a baseline of the kinds of activities that take place in the family and then develop goals and design strategies that will help the family meet the goals. Reinforce the new ways of relating in the family.

44. Relative to multicultural issues, which is *not* important in family counseling (p. 166)? (www)
   <u>a.</u> The importance of teaching the family about majority values in order for them to better understand how their issues play out in the "real world."
   b. A focus on external factors like racism and poverty
   c. Understanding the bicultural nature of many minorities
   d. Understanding the different world views of minority families
   e. Understanding that language differences may cause communication problems between the therapist and family
   f. None of the above (all are important)

45. Which of the following is always unethical in family counseling (p. 167)?
   <u>a.</u> Not having each family member giving informed consent for treatment
   b. Withholding treatment of one family member in order to see the whole family
   c. Seeing a family member in individual counseling and then at a later date seeing the whole family
   d. Not guaranteeing the confidential nature of the relationship as members of the family sometimes will reveal information outside of the sessions
   e. None of the above (all are ethical)

46. Which of the following accredits marriage and family counseling programs (p. 168)?

a. ACA	d. IAMFC	g. a and d
b. CACREP	e. a and b	h. b and d
c. CAMFTE	<u>f.</u> b and c	i. c and d

<u>True or False</u>

47. Divorce is the systems response to stress that cannot be resolved (p. 151) (**T**).

48. The concept that the same endpoint can be reached from a number of starting points is called equifinality (p. 153) (**T**).

49. One cannot not communicate (p. 157) (**T**).

50. Digital communication is the meaning about communication, analogic communication is the exact words that the message implies (p. 157) (**F**).

51. Haley suggests that advice giving is often an effective way to give directives (pp. 158-159) (**F**).

52. The ultimate goal of therapy for Murray Bowen is the development of a healthy ego (pp. 161-162) (**T**).

53. Carl Whitaker's negation of theory is *not* evident when you examine how he actually worked (pp. 163-164) (**T**).

54. Behavioral family therapists tend to focus more on non-linear thinking than individually oriented behavioral therapists (p. 165) (**T**).

55. As opposed to individually oriented behavior therapy, because of its very nature, behavioral family therapy has to focus on underlying issues and intrapsychic processes (pp. 165-166) (**F**).

56. Psychodynamic family therapy tends to be a very slow process, much like individually oriented psychodynamic approaches (pp. 164-165) (**F**).

57. It is rarely if ever ethical to withhold treatment from one member of a family in order to see the whole family (p. 167) (**F**).

58. Interpersonal and intrapsychic forces play a much more important role in working with minority families than do external factors such as poverty and racism (pp. 166-167) (**F**).

59. One method of obtaining payment from families in this time of limited insurance payments is to rotate the submission of each family member's insurance form (p. 169) (**F**).

60. A family member can never testify against another family member about what he or she learned in a family counseling session (p. 169) (**F**).

61. It is ethical and legal for a counselor to bill for individual counseling because the insurance company will not pay for family counseling (pp. 166-167). (**F**)

<u>INFOTRAC KEY WORDS:</u> Ethics in marriage therapy. Family development. Family transitions. Family therapy.

CHAPTER 7

GROUP WORK

Multiple Choice

1. Which of the following is *not* an advantage of group counseling over individual counseling (p. 174)?
   a. More economical
   b. Greater ability to develop a sense of belonging
   c. Groups represent a microcosm of society
   d. Groups generally offer a safer atmosphere in which to open up
   e. Vicarious learning can occur in groups

2. Prior to 1900 the purpose of group treatment was (p. 174): (www)
   a. to assist individuals in very functional and pragmatic ways
   b. to provide an outlet for emotional problems
   c. to discuss group dynamics and power issues in groups
   d. to examine intrapsychic issues
   e. Two of the above

3. Which of the following was *not* responsible for the development of group work (p. 175)?
   a. Moralistic group discussions with individuals who were poor
   b. The vocational guidance movement
   c. Early theorizing about group dynamics by such individuals like Freud
   d. The development of group treatment for individuals who were ill
   e. None of the above (all were responsible)

4. Relative to the origins of group work, which of the following theoretical concepts were *not* popular at the beginning of the twentieth century (pp. 175-176)?
   a. The herd instinct: the concept that people generally flock toward one another
   b. The concept that people would sometimes act out aggressively in groups
   c. The concept that issues of race and gender play an important part in group dynamics
   d. The idea that individuals tend to give their power over to the leader
   e. None of the above (all occurred during this time period)

5. Which of the following was the originator of psychodrama and is given the credit for coining the term *group psychotherapy* (p. 175)?
   a. Freud **b.** Moreno c. Lewin d. Rogers

6. Relative to group work, which did *not* occur during the 1920s and 1930s (p. 175)?
   a. The inclusion of existential-humanistic philosophy in group work
   b. The inclusion of Adlerian theory in group work
   c. The spread of group guidance activities
   d. The first professional associations related to group work
   e. None of the above (all occurred during this time period)

7. Relative to group work, the 1940s were highlighted by all but which of the following (p. 176)?
   a. The development of the National Training Laboratory (NTL)
   b. A focus on group dynamics and the intricate ways in which people in groups interact
   c. The first encounter groups
   d. The spread of groups with varying theoretical orientations
   e. None of the above (all occurred during this time period)

8. Relative to group work, the 1960s were highlighted by all but which of the following (pp. 176-177)?
   a. The spread of the encounter group movement
   b. The establishment of Esalen and other experimental communities
   c. A strong focus on feelings in much of the group work being conducted
   d. The establishment of the Association for Specialists in Group Work (ASGW)
   e. The spread of groups with varying theoretical orientations
   f. None of the above (all occurred during this time period)

9. Recent trends in group work include all but which of the following (p. 177)?
   a. The spread of group course work in training programs
   b. A decline in some of the more outrageous groups of the past
   c. The spread of common-theme groups and brief-counseling groups
   d. The spread of self-help groups
   e. The spread of training standards and ethical guidelines
   f. None of the above (all are recent trends)

10. The following statement refers to which of the terms listed below (p. 178)?
"The changes that occur in a group as a function of the developmental stages through which the group will pass."
   a. Group dynamics b. Group work **c.** Group process d. Group counseling

11. The following statement refers to which of the terms listed below (p. 178)?
" The ongoing interactions and interrelationships among the members of the group and between the leader and the members of the group"
   a. Group dynamics b. Group work c. Group process d. Group counseling

12. Groups whose purpose is to educate, affirm, and enhance members' strengths and generally have a volunteer leader are called which of the following (p. 178)? (www)
   a. Brief-counseling groups d. Common-theme groups g. Therapy groups
   b. Self-help groups e. Task groups
   c. Psychoeducational groups f. Counseling groups

13. Groups that emphasize conscious behaviors, focus on group dynamics and the successful completion of a product are called which of the following (p. 180)?
   a. Brief-counseling groups d. Common-theme groups g. Therapy groups
   b. Self-help groups **e.** Task groups
   c. Psychoeducational groups f. Counseling groups

14. Groups whose goals are to prevent an array of educational and psychological disturbances and have a well-trained leader are called which of the following (p. 180)?
   a. Brief-counseling groups d. Common-theme groups g. Therapy groups
   b. Self-help groups e. Task groups
   c. Psychoeducational groups f. Counseling groups

15. Groups that seek to help members resolve problems of living through interpersonal support and problem solving and who have a well-trained leader are called which of the following (p. 181)?
   a. Brief-counseling groups d. Common-theme groups g. Therapy groups
   b. Self-help groups e. Task groups
   c. Psychoeducational groups **f.** Counseling groups

16. Groups that focus on a specialized topic, are generally short-term, and have a well-trained leader are called which of the following (p. 182)?
   a. Brief-counseling groups **d.** Common-theme groups g. Therapy groups
   b. Self-help groups e. Task groups
   c. Psychoeducational groups f. Counseling groups

17. Groups that are time-limited, usually less than 20 sessions and are focused, structured, action oriented, and have a highly trained leader are called which of the following (p. 182)?
   a. Brief-counseling groups d. Common-theme groups g. Therapy groups
   b. Self-help groups e. Task groups
   c. Psychoeducational groups f. Counseling groups

18. Groups that seek to remediate in-depth psychological problems are called which of the following (p. 182)?
   a. Brief-counseling groups d. Common-theme groups **g.** Therapy groups
   b. Self-help groups e. Task groups
   c. Psychoeducational groups f. Counseling groups

19. Alcoholics Anonymous is an example of what type of group (p. 178)?
 a. Brief-counseling groups
 b. Self-help groups
 c. Psychoeducational groups
 d. Common-theme groups
 e. Task groups
 f. Counseling groups
 g. Therapy groups

20. Some advantages to psychoanalytic group therapy over traditional psychoanalysis include all but which of the following (pp. 184-185)? (www)
 a. The shear number of individuals in a group allow for more opportunity to recreate past family issues through transference
 b. There is increased opportunity for feedback concerning defenses and resistances
 c. There is less chance of extreme dependency on the therapist
 d. Seeing others work through similar issues helps to reduce defensiveness
 e. The same techniques used in individual work can be easily applied to group work

21. A theoretical approach to group work which focuses on re-creating, analyzing, discussing, and interpreting past experiences and working through defenses and resistances is which of the following (pp. 184-185)?
 a. Person-centered group therapy
 b. Rational-emotive-behavior group therapy
 c. Behavioral group therapy
 d. Psychoanalytic group therapy
 e. None of the above

22. Some advantages to behavioral group therapy over individual behavioral therapy include all but which of the following (pp. 185-186)?
 a. The establishment of group cohesion allows quick feedback concerning problem identification and strategies for change from other group members
 b. Reinforcement of the changes made can occur among group members
 c. A group member can rehearse new behaviors in the group prior to trying them in the "real world"
 d. Group members can act as models for other group members, thereby offering more opportunity to learn from others
 e. The projection of unconscious processes allows group members to target new behaviors for change

23. A theoretical approach to group work which focuses on building trust and group cohesion, targeting specific behaviors for change, and working on the change process is called which of the following (pp. 185-186)?
 a. Person-centered group therapy
 b. Rational-emotive-behavior group therapy
 c. Behavioral group therapy
 d. Psychoanalytic group therapy
 e. None of the above

24. Some advantages of group REBT over individual REBT includes all but which of the following (pp. 186-187)?
 a. Group members can challenge one another to think and act differently
 b. Group members can practice news ways of acting in front of each other
 c. As a result of the group process, there is a great possibility of building a warm relationship with the leader
 d. Members can obtain reinforcement from one another for taking on a more rational way of living
 e. Members can encourage one another to continue to dispute irrational beliefs and take on new behaviors after initial changes have been made

25. A theoretical approach to group work which has an active, directive, and confrontational leader who focuses on getting members to take on a new philosophy of living is called which of the following (pp. 186-187)?
 a. Person-centered group therapy
 b. Rational-emotive-behavior group therapy
 c. Behavioral group therapy
 d. Psychoanalytic group therapy
 e. None of the above

26. Some advantages of person-centered group counseling over person-centered individual counseling includes all but which of the following (pp. 187-188)?
   a. Members are able to surrender to the healing that takes place in the group process
   b. Members can receive feedback and be confronted by others, thus leading to a cracking of facades
   c. Members can have an opportunity to develop deep relationships with others that can be a model for other relationships
   d. As a result of group cohesion members are able to give their power over to the leader and let that person target specific behaviors for change

27. A theoretical approach to group work which downplays unconscious motivations and believes in the ability of the individual to increase his or her self-awareness and insight as a natural function of the group process is called which of the following (pp. 187-188)?
   a. Person-centered group therapy
   b. Rational-emotive-behavior group therapy
   c. Behavioral group therapy
   d. Psychoanalytic group therapy
   e. None of the above

28. Issues of group composition, whether the group is open or closed, the size and duration of the groups, the frequency of meetings, and securing a place to meet are all part of (p. 188):
   a. the pregroup stage
   b. the initial stage
   c. preparing for the group
   d. None of the above

29. Identifying the needs, expectations, and commitment of group members; challenging myths and misconceptions, conveying and procuring information, and screening potential members are all part of (p. 190):
   a. the pregroup stage
   b. the initial stage
   c. preparing for the group
   d. None of the above

30. Which group stage is highlighted by anxiety, apprehension, and issues of trust (p. 190)? (www)
   a. Pregroup **b.** Initial c. Transition d. Work e. Closure

31. Which group stage is highlighted by issues of control, power, and authority (p. 190)?
   a. Pregroup b. Initial **c.** Transition d. Work e. Closure

32. At the end of which stage do group members begin to transition to a "calmer place," are able to talk about their feelings, and take responsibility for self (pp. 190-191)?
   a. Pregroup b. Initial **c.** Transition d. Work e. Closure

33. In which stage is there a deepening of trust, a sense of cohesion, relative ease at giving feedback, and the setting of goals (pp. 191-192)?
   a. Pregroup b. Initial c. Transition **d.** Work e. Closure

34. Which stage is highlighted by a sense of accomplishment, high self-esteem, and a sense of completion (p. 192)?
   a. Pregroup b. Initial c. Transition d. Work **e.** Closure

35. In this stage important leadership skills include setting limits, showing empathy and positive regard, and staying cognizant of possible scapegoating (p. 190).
   a. Pregroup **b.** Initial c. Transition d. Work e. Closure

36. In this stage important leadership skills include showing empathy and positive regard, actively preventing scapegoating, and assuring that anger doesn't get out of hand (pp. 190-191).
   a. Pregroup b. Initial **c.** Transition d. Work e. Closure

37. In this stage important leadership skills could include support and confrontation, higher-level empathy, probing questions, and interpretation (pp. 191-192).
   a. Pregroup b. Initial c. Transition **d.** Work e. Closure

38. Leadership skills in this stage include summarizing accomplishments, using empathy to deal with bereavement issues, and facilitating sharing of feelings among group members (p. 192).
   a. Pregroup b. Initial c. Transition d. Work **e.** Closure

39. At the very minimum, when giving informed consent, group members should have all but which of the following (p. 194)?
   a. The credentials of the group leader
   b. The therapeutic style of the group leader
   c. A pregroup interview to determine the appropriateness of the group
   d. The groundrules of the group
   e. Expectations about self-disclosure, confidentiality, and psychological risks
   f. A clear indication of what should be talked about

40. It might be wise to refer a client to a group when (pp. 194-195): (www)
   a. a client cannot afford individual counseling
   b. clients' issues are mostly related to interpersonal issues
   c. a client needs social support
   d. the experiences of others will assist the client
   e. a client wants to test out new behaviors in a relatively safe setting
   f. a client, who is in individual counseling, believes he or she will profit from also seeing the same therapist in group counseling
   g. all of the above

True or False

41. A group has many of the same dynamics of a family (p. 173) (T).

42. The third-party rule states that individuals who are privy to information revealed to more than one person (e.g., a group) have a right to keep that information confidential (p. 195) (F).

43. If a group is to proceed, group leaders must be able to assure that everything said in a group is kept confidential (p. 194) (F).

44. Because the theoretical orientation of the leader varies so dramatically, group process issues will vary dramatically from group to group (p. 192) (F).

45. The kinds of techniques used will be partly based on the stage of the group and the theoretical orientation of the leader (p. 192) (T).

46. Because issues of deep-seated racism are likely to occur in a culturally diverse group, it is often recommended that groups are culturally homogenous (p. 193) (F).

47. The difference between a counseling and therapy group is a matter of degree of intensity rather than major differences in technique and philosophy (pp. 181-183) (T).

48. The difference between psychoeducational groups and counseling groups is minimal, if at all (p. 183) (F).

49. Most theories of counseling have been applied to group work (p. 184) (T).

50. Many individual theories of counseling have been adapted to group work by explaining how the group process and group dynamics can be used with the theory (p. 184) (F).

51. The ACA division that focuses on group work is called the Association of Specialists in Group Work (ASGW) (p. 195) (T).

INFOTRAC KEY WORDS: Trust and group counseling. Preparation and group counseling. Group and elderly. Group and children. Multicultural and group.

CHAPTER 8
CONSULTATION AND SUPERVISION

Multiple Choice

1. Consultation is a (p. 199):
   a. dyadic relationship
   b. triadic relationship
   c. systemic relationship
   d. none of the above

2. Which decades are generally identified as the beginning of modern-day consultation (p. 200)?
   a. 1890s and 1900s b. 1920s and 1930s c. 1940s and 1950s d. 1960s and 1970s

3. Early consultation was called which of the following (p. 200)? (www)
   a. The direct-service approach
   b. Consultant-centered consultation
   c. System-centered consultation
   d. Process-oriented consultation

4. The direct-service approach to consultation viewed the consultant as a(n) (p. 200):
   a. collaborator to discuss the problem
   b. facilitator to assist in solving the problem
   c. counselor to listen about the problem
   d. expert to solve the problem

5. The 1950s and 1960s saw the consultant as a(n) (p. 200):
   a. trainer, who was an expert in problem solving and would educate staff about problem areas
   b. problem-solver, who came in and solved the problem
   c. counselor, who would facilitate listening skills among different levels of the organization
   d. collaborator, who would collaborate with the head of an organization and assist in problem solving

6. Which decade saw expanded versions of old models and the development of new models (pp. 200-201)?
   a. 1920s and 1930s b. 1940s and 1950s c. 1970s d. 1980s

7. Two recent trends in consultation include which of the following (p. 201)?
   a. A focus on developmental theory and counseling theories
   b. A focus on systemic thinking and a developmental perspective
   c. Primary and tertiary prevention
   d. Viewing the consultant as expert
   e. All of the above

8. A consultant who has multiple ways of viewing a problem is one who is a (p. 201):
   a. systemic thinker
   b. multiplistic thinker
   c. expert consultant
   d. modern-day consultant

9. Consultant-centered consultation includes all but which of the following (p. 202)?
   a. Expert consultant
   b. Prescriptive consultant
   c. Trainer and/or educator
   d. Process-oriented consultant

10. System-centered consultation includes all but which of the following (p. 203)?
    a. Consultant negotiator and/or facilitator
    b. Trainer and/or educator
    c. Consultant as collaborator
    d. Process-oriented consultant

11. The expert consultant (p. 202):
   a. is responsible for coming into the system and finding a "cure"
   b. collects information, diagnoses the problem, and makes recommendations to the consultee on how to solve the problem
   c. comes into a system to teach or train the staff
   d. helps individuals within the system communicate with one another, understand each other, and resolve conflicts among themselves
   e. acts as a facilitator of the change process by working jointly with the individuals involved
   f. believes that either he or she does not have the "answer" or withholds his or her expertise with the belief that the most effective resolution comes from members finding their own solution

12. The consultant negotiator and/or facilitator (p. 202): (www)
   a. is responsible for coming into the system and finding a "cure"
   b. collects information, diagnoses the problem, and makes recommendations to the consultee on how to solve the problem
   c. comes into a system to teach or train the staff
   d. helps individuals within the system communicate with one another, understand each other, and resolve conflicts among themselves
   e. acts as a facilitator of the change process by working jointly with the individuals involved
   f. believes that either he or she does not have the "answer" or withholds his or her expertise with the belief that the most effective resolution comes from members finding their own solution

13. The consultant as collaborator (p. 203):
   a. is responsible for coming into the system and finding a "cure"
   b. collects information, diagnoses the problem, and makes recommendations to the consultee on how to solve the problem
   c. comes into a system to teach or train the staff
   d. helps individuals within the system communicate with one another, understand each other, and resolve conflicts among themselves
   e. acts as a facilitator of the change process by working jointly with the individuals involved
   f. believes that either he or she does not have the "answer" or withholds his or her expertise with the belief that the most effective resolution comes from members finding their own solution

14. The process-oriented consultant (p.203):
   a. is responsible for coming into the system and finding a "cure"
   b. collects information, diagnoses the problem, and makes recommendations to the consultee on how to solve the problem
   c. comes into a system to teach or train the staff
   d. helps individuals within the system communicate with one another, understand each other, and resolve conflicts among themselves
   e. acts as a facilitator of the change process by working jointly with the individuals involved
   f. believes that either he or she does not have the "answer" or withholds his or her expertise with the belief that the most effective resolution comes from members finding their own solution

15. The prescriptive consultant (p. 202):
   a. is responsible for coming into the system and finding a "cure"
   b. collects information, diagnoses the problem, and makes recommendations to the consultee on how to solve the problem
   c. comes into a system to teach or train the staff
   d. helps individuals within the system communicate with one another, understand each other, and resolve conflicts among themselves
   e. acts as a facilitator of the change process by working jointly with the individuals involved
   f. believes that either he or she does not have the "answer" or withholds his or her expertise with the belief that the most effective resolution comes from members finding their own solution

16. The consultant who is a trainer and/or educator (p. 202):
    a. is responsible for coming into the system and finding a "cure"
    b. collects information, diagnoses the problem, and makes recommendations to the consultee on how to solve the problem
    c. comes into a system to teach or train the staff
    d. helps individuals within the system communicate with one another, understand each other, and resolve conflicts among themselves
    e. acts as a facilitator of the change process by working jointly with the individuals involved
    f. believes that either he or she does not have the "answer" or withholds his or her expertise with the belief that the most effective resolution comes from members finding their own solution

17. Which theory of consultation stresses the importance of expression of feeling and the letting down of boundaries in an effort to promote increased awareness and encounters with one another (p. 204)?
    a. Person-centered consultation
    b. Gestalt consultation
    c. Learning theory consultation
    d. Psychoanalytic consultation
    e. Chaos theory consultation

18. Which theory of consultation attempts to understand each person's perspective on the nature of the system and run groups in order to help individuals hear one another in the belief that the natural process of the group will help heal the system (p. 203)?
    a. Person-centered consultation
    b. Gestalt consultation
    c. Learning theory consultation
    d. Psychoanalytic consultation
    e. Chaos theory consultation

19. Which theory of consultation stresses identifying problem areas and setting goals and strategies for change based on these problem areas (p. 203)? (www)
    a. Person-centered consultation
    b. Gestalt consultation
    c. Learning theory consultation
    d. Psychoanalytic consultation
    e. Chaos theory consultation

20. Which theory of consultation examines how unconscious behaviors affect the consulting environment and who attempts to discern how these unconscious forces manifest problems (p. 203)?
    a. Person-centered consultation
    b. Gestalt consultation
    c. Learning theory consultation
    d. Psychoanalytic consultation
    e. Chaos theory consultation

21. Which theory of consultation assumes that systems are affected by a vast number of factors and the role of the consultant is to understand as many of those factors as possible (p. 204)?
    a. Person-centered consultation
    b. Gestalt consultation
    c. Learning theory consultation
    d. Psychoanalytic consultation
    e. Chaos theory consultation

22. Some examples of consultation by college counseling center staff includes all but which of the following (p. 207)?
    a. Meeting with faculty concerning the emotional distresses of college students
    b. Meeting with administrators over diversity issues on campus
    c. Reaching out to students so that they might attend group counseling sessions
    d. Having individuals from academic advising discuss issues related to high risk students
    e. Meeting with directors of residence life to analyze the potential psychological stressors of students

23. When the focus of consultation is on assisting individuals who have some mental health concerns but are not clients directly involved with the agency it is called which of the following (p. 208)?
    a. Systemic consultation
    b. Process-oriented consultation
    c. Collaborative consultation
    d. Consulting outward

24. Gerald Caplan's theory of consultation has generally been applied in which of the following settings (p. 208)? (www)
   a. Schools b. Business and Industry c. Colleges **d.** Agencies

25. With which of the following does the school counselor *not* consult (p. 210)?
   a. Students
   b. Administrators
   c. Professionals in the community
   d. Teachers
   e. Parents
   f. None of the above (they consult with all of these)

26. Supervision differs from consultation in all of the following ways except which of the following (p. 211)?
   a. Supervision involves a more intense relationship than consultation
   b. Supervision involves a direct evaluative relationship, consultation generally does not
   c. Supervision involves an ongoing relationship, consultation generally does not
   d. Supervision affects only one person, consultation affects many

27. Parallel process in involves which of the following (p. 212)?
   a. The manner in which a supervisory relationship may mimic a counseling relationship
   b. The manner in which a consultative relationship my mimic administrative relationships
   c. The way that clients tend to offer parallel explanations to life dilemmas
   d. The manner in which similar problems tend to reverberate through a system

28. Which of the following is not a model of supervision (pp. 213-214)? (www)
   a. Developmental models
   b. Integrated models
   c. Eclectic models
   d. Orientation-specific models

29. Stoltenberg and Delworth's model of supervision states that supervisees tend to (p. 214):
   a. become increasingly aware of client needs and the interventions that might suit them
   b. become less dependent on the supervisor as they gain faith in their own ability
   c. at first feel very enthusiastic, later feel less so, and later again feeling motivated
   d. at first feel apprehensive and lack of enthusiasm, and later become motivated and enthusiastic
   e. two of the above
   f. three of the above
   g. all of the above

30. Stoltenberg and Delworth's model of supervision is considered (p 214):
   a. a developmental model
   b. an orientation-specific model
   c. an eclectic model
   d. an integrated model

31. Bernard's model of supervision is considered (p 215: (www)
   a. a developmental model
   b. an orientation-specific model
   c. an eclectic model
   d. an integrated model

32. Kegan's Interpersonal Process Recall (IPR) model of supervision is considered (p. 216):
   a. A developmental model
   b. An orientation-specific model
   c. An eclectic model
   d. An integrated model

33. Which of the following describe orientation-specific models of supervision (pp. 214-215)?
   a. When the supervisor structures supervision so that it models a particular approach that the supervisee is using
   b. When the supervisor uses his or her knowledge base to gently guide and teach the supervisee
   c. When the supervisee designates an orientation to follow and the supervisor gives critical feedback about the supervisees ability
   d. When the supervisor designates an orientation to the supervisee which the supervise must follow
   e. a and b
   f. c and d
   g. All of the above

34. Bernard's discrimination model of supervision includes all but which of the following (pp. 215-216)?
   a. A didactic role in which the supervisor is a teacher
   b. A role in which the supervisor attempts to discriminate one theoretical approach from another for the supervisee
   c. An experiential role in which the supervisor takes on the role of a "limited" counselor
   d. The role of a consultant, in which the supervisor is an objective "colleague"

35. Kagan's Interpersonal Process Recall (IPR) model of supervision (p. 216):
   a. allows the supervisee to uncover his or her own strengths and weakneeses
   b. follows in the humanistic tradition
   c. is a cross between the psychoanalytic tradition and humanistic tradition
   d. a and b
   e. a and c

36. Which of the following has been shown to *not* be useful as a means for obtaining supervisor feedback (p. 217)?
   a. Telephone calls during sessions
   b. The use of a ear phone
   c. The use of a computer where supervisors can type in feedback to the supervisee
   d. The use of e-mail
   e. The use of real-time video links
   f. All of the above have been shown to be useful

True/False

37. It is often suggested that consultants and supervisors avoid cross-cultural consultation/ supervisory relationships because of the inherent bias in them (pp. 218-219) **(F)**.

38. The same standard regarding sexual relationships with clients is not applied to supervisory relationships because they involve an interpersonal relationship of less intensity (p. 219) **(F)**.

39. ACES has developed standards of supervision which have eleven core areas (p. 219) **(T)**.

40. The values of the consultant and supervisor plays a small role in the consultation and supervisory relationships (p. 220) **(F)**.

41. Because of the "second-tier relationship" of supervisors and consultants, they hold little liability for actions related to their supervisees of consultees (p. 220) **(F)**.

42. Tatiana Tarasoff's parents sued the supervisor of the psychologist for negligence and won their suit, thus highlighting the importance of the role supervisors play in the relationship between counselor and client (p. 220) **(T)**.

43. Because of the numbers of people involved in consulting, informed consent need not be obtained (p. 220) **(F)**.

44. Because of the numbers of people involved in consulting, confidentiality plays a small role in the relationship between the consultant and members of an organization (p. 219) **(F)**.

45. Up to 45% of school counselors receive no supervision whatsoever (p. 217) **(T)**.

46. One well-known developmental model of supervision was devised by Norm Kagan (p. 216) **(F)**.

47. The benefits of individual supervision are such that it is generally recommended over group supervision (p. 213) **(F)**.

48. Consultation for the school counselor tends to be a little less precarious than for the college counselor or agency counselor (p. 196) **(F)**.

49. One major responsibility of the supervisor is the welfare of the supervisees clients (p. 197) **(T)**.

50. Consultation in the schools is one of the main functions of the school counselor (pp. 209-210) (**T**).

51. The original Community Mental Health Centers Act of 1963 did not highlight consultation as one of the major services offered by mental health centers (p. 208) (**F**).

52. Consultation by college counselors may be defined as any activity where in-depth counseling is offered to a group, office, department, or club (p. 207) (**F**).

53. Theories provide a conceptual framework for consultation, models suggests a style of consultation that speaks to how the consultant brings him or herself into the consulting relationship (p. 203) (**T**).

54. The theoretical orientation of the consultant is rarely related to the consultant's style or model of consultation (p. 203) (**F**).

55. The consulting process consists of four stages which beings with initial contact, intervention selection, evaluation, and termination (p. 205) (**F**).

56. The solution searching and intervention selection stage of the consulting process should only occur after a thorough analysis of problems in the system (p. 206) (**T**).

57. Outreach is a form of consultation (p. 207) (**F**).

58. Over the years the literature on consultation has improved to the point where there is now a universally accepted definition of consultation (p. 199) (**F**).

INFOTRAC KEY WORDS: Consultation model. Consultation theory. Ethical clinical superv. Legal clinical superv. Models of supervision.

CHAPTER 9

DEVELOPMENT ACROSS THE LIFEPSAN

Multiple Choice

1. During which decade did "development" become more than a catchword, and became truly established in the counseling profession (p. 225)?
   a. The 1950s <u>d.</u> The 1980s
   b. The 1960s e. The 1990s
   c. The 1970s f. None of the above

2. Which of the following is *not* a characteristic of human development (pp. 226-227)?
   a. Development builds upon itself and is orderly
   b. Development is painful, yet growth producing
   c. Developmental models are transtheoretical
   d. Development, by its very nature is predictable
   <u>e.</u> Incompletion of stage-specific tasks never leads to pathology
   f. Knowledge of development lends itself to a preventive, wellness model of the person

3. Arnold Gesell has described (p. 228): (www)
   a. A cognitive development theory
   <u>b.</u> The normative physical growth and social development process for children
   c. A moral development theory
   d. All of the above

4. Knowledge of development by a counselor can do all but which of the following (pp. 245-246):
   a. Alert counselors to developmental lags
   b. Assist individuals through predictable transitions
   c. Help assess possible abuse or neglect of children
   d. Help counselors have greater empathy for their clients
   <u>e.</u> All of the above

5. Joyce sees a tall thin glass of water and thinks that it has more volume than a short wide glass (although each hold the same amount of water). Joyce is in which of Piaget's stages (p. 231)?
   a. Formal operational c. Sensorimotor
   b. Concrete operational <u>d.</u> Preoperational

6. Mary can figure things out through a series of logical tasks but cannot deal with hypothetical situations. She is in which of Piaget stages (p. 232)?
   a. Formal operational c. Sensorimotor
   <u>b.</u> Concrete operational d. Preoperational

7. Assimilation refers to which of the following(p. 231?
   <u>a.</u> When a child uses his or her existing way of understanding the world to make sense out of new knowledge.
   b. How a person changes his or her previous ways of knowing to make sense out of new knowledge
   c. How new cognitive structures are formed
   d. Two of the above

8. The word that best describes new cognitive structures, or new ways of thinking that are developed as we learn is (p. 231):
   a. Assimilation b. Accommodation <u>c.</u> Schemata d. Ego

9. Despite the fact that her family is starving, a mother decides not to steal food from a supermarket because this would be against societal rules. This adult is in which of Kohlberg's levels (p. 232)?
   a. Preconventional <u>b.</u> Conventional c. Postconventional d. Postformal

10. Chucky wants to steal a cookie from the refrigerator when his mother isn't looking, but doesn't do so for fear of being disciplined. Which of Kohlberg's levels is Chucky probably in (p. 232)?
   a. Preconventional   b. Conventional   c. Postconventional   d. Postformal

11. Which is true about Carol Gilligan's concept of moral development as compared to Kohlberg's (pp. 234-235)?
   a. Women, as compared to men, will tend to stress interdependence more than autonomy at the higher levels of development.
   b. Some women may be viewed by Kohlberg at lower levels of moral development because they do not stress autonomy as much as men.
   c. Women stress a "standard of caring" in making moral decisions, men do not.
   d. a and b
   e. All of the above

12. A child who has little control of his or her actions is in which of Kegan's stages (p. 236)? (www)
   a. Interindividual   d. Interpersonal
   b. Impulsive   e. Incorporative
   c. Imperial   f. Imperial

13. An adult who can hear feedback from others and has mutuality in his or her relationships is in which of Kegan's stages (p. 237)?
   a. Interindividual   d. Interpersonal
   b. Impulsive   e. Incorporative
   c. Imperial   f. Imperial

14. According to Kegan's constructivist view of adult cognitive development, a person who is embedded in her or his relationships is in what stage (p. 237)?
   a. Interindividual Stage   c. Interpersonal Stage
   b. Institutional Stage   d. None of the above

15. According to Kegan's constructivist view of adult cognitive development, a person who has separated his or her values and sense of self from parents, peers, and/or community groups can be in which of the following stage(s) (p. 237).?
   a. Interindividual Stage   c. Interpersonal Stage
   b. Institutional Stage   d. None of the above

16. According to William Perry's theory, a person who thinks in terms of right or wrong would be in which stage of development (p. 238)?
   a. Dualism   c. Relativism
   b. Commitment to relativism   d. None of the above

17. According to William Perry, a person in the "commitment to relativism" stage will do all but which of the following (p. 238)?
   a. Seldom take a stand on an issue   d. Commit to specific values and behaviors.
   b. Think abstractly   e. None of the above (this individual will do all of the above)
   c. Allow for differing opinions

18. Which of the following is considered a theory of adult cognitive development (p. 235)?
   a. Piaget's theory of cognitive development
   b. Levinson's theory of men's development
   c. Erikson's theory of psychosocial development
   d. Kegan's theory of constructive development
   e. Two of the above
   f. Three of the above
   g. All of the above

19. Which of the following is considered a theory of lifespan development (p. 241)? (www)
    a. Piaget's theory of cognitive development
    b. Levinson's theory of men's development
    c. Erikson's theory of psychosocial development
    d. Kegan's theory of constructive development
    e. Two of the above
    f. Three of the above
    g. All of the above

20. The Eriksonian stage which occurs in adolescence is which of the following (p. 241)?
    a. Initiative vs. guilt
    b. Trust vs. mistrust
    c. Industry vs. inferiority
    d. Identify vs. role confusion

21. The Eriksonian issue which occurs in middle-life is which of the following (p. 241)? (www)
    a. Generativity vs. stagnation
    b. Intimacy vs. isolation
    c. Industry vs. inferiority
    d. Identify vs. role confusion

22. Juan's parents are constantly praising him for trying out new activities. Juan, who is in preschool, thus feels adventurous and has high self-esteem. Which Eriksonian stage is Juan in (p. 241)?
    a. Initiative vs. guilt
    b. Trust vs. mistrust
    c. Industry vs. inferiority
    d. Identify vs. role confusion

23. Levinson's concept of *life structures* refers to all but which of the following (p. 242)?
    a. Intellectual development
    b. Career development
    c. Love relationships
    d. Marriage and family
    e. Relationship with self
    f. Role of self in social context
    g. Relationships with individuals, groups, and institutions

24. In which of Levinson's eras is their a reappraisal and modification of one's life (p. 242)?
    a. Childhood and adolescence
    b. Early adulthood
    c. Middle adulthood
    d. Late adulthood

25. In Fowler's theory of faith development, which of the following is an aspect of how faith is defined (p. 243)?
    a. A person's core values
    b. The images of power that drive a person
    c. The stories that drive a person consciously and unconsciously
    d. The ways we make meaning
    e. a and d
    f. b and c
    g. All of the above

26. Intuitive-projective faith is which of the following (p. 243)?
    a. When a person projects his or her faith experience on others and believes that the other person shares a similar belief
    b. A young child's illogical belief in stories and myths which can be affected by adult views of faith
    c. A deep respect for the faith experience of others and a sense of humility regarding all that is known
    d. An integration of many points of view and an acceptance of the faith experience of others

27. Forty-five-year-old Jill has spent much of her adult life exploring different experiences of faith and has gained a deep acceptance of varying points of view. In addition, she has come to integrate different points of view into her own faith experience. In which of Fowler stages is she (p. 245)?
    a. Primary faith
    b. Intuitive-projective faith
    c. Mythic-literal faith
    d. Syntheic-conventional faith
    e. Individuative-reflexive faith
    f. Paradoxical-conjunctive faith
    g. Universalizing faith

28. Twelve-year-old Anton believes that his religion is the "right " religion. Although he has the ability to think abstractly about other faith experiences, his limited exposure to other religions continues to reinforce his beliefs about his religion. He is in which of Fowler's stages (p. 244)?
   a. Primary faith
   b. Intuitive-projective faith
   c. Mythic-literal faith
   d. Synthetic-conventional faith
   e. Individuative-reflexive faith
   f. Paradoxical-conjunctive faith
   g. Universalizing faith

29. Which of the following has sometimes been true of counselors (p. 248)? (www)
   a. Because they are so developmentally focused, they sometimes miss serious pathology
   b. Because they are so focused on pathology, they tend to label and box people into diagnostic categories
   c. They are sometimes fearful of looking at the dark side of people
   d. Two of the above
   e. None of the above

30. Which of the following divisions of ACA focus upon issues of development (p. 248)?
   a. AADA and C-AHEAD
   b. ACES and IAAOC
   c. IAMFC and AMCD
   d. AADA and ACES
   e. IAAOC and AMCD
   f. C-AHEAD and IAAOC

True or False

31. The scope and rate of the physical development of a child is fairly consistent (p. 228) **(F)**.

32. Because children do develop at unpredictable rates, norm group comparisons are not particularly useful (p. 228) **(F)**.

33. Since development is so unpredictable, it is nearly impossible to develop helping strategies based on a client's developmental level (p. 228) **(F)**.

34. Piaget's concept of schemata refers to how a person changes his or her previous ways of knowing to make sense out of new knowledge (p. 231) **(F)**.

35. Piaget's formal operations stage is marked by the ability to think abstractly and apply more complex levels of knowing (p. 232) **(T)**.

36. According to Kohlberg's theory, people at the conventional level make moral decisions based upon universal truths, abd moral values and principles of the individual, rather than upon societal standards (p. 232) **(F)**.

37. Gilligan found that moral reasoning in women differed from that of men in that women value having the freedom to make choices, while men value connectedness (p. 234) **(F)**.

38. There is a relationship between cognitive development and moral development (p. 235) **(T)**.

39. It is theoretically inconsistent for a person who is in Piaget's concrete-operational stage to be a postconventional thinker (p. 235) **(T)**.

40. Kegan's theory of constructive developmental is also called subject/object theory (p. 235) **(T)**.

41. If a person is to full reach the higher levels of Kegan and Perry's stages of cognitive development, he or she is most likely over forty years old (p. 247) **(T)**.

42. Perry's theory of empistemological reflection has largely been applied to children (p. 238) **(F)**.

43. Harold Mathews is a seventy-year-old retired military officer. He looks back at his life and feels distraught. He probably is experiencing Erikson's "Stagnation" stage (pp. 240-241) **(F)**.

44. In Levinson's theory, eras subdivided into periods are preceded by transitional periods (p. 241) **(T)**.

45. An infant's ability to trust early on in life is the basis for his or her later development of faith, says Fowler (p. 243) (**T**).

46. Fowler believes an atheist can have faith (p. 243) (**T**).

47. Fowler's concept of "decentration from self"is when a person is out of touch with his or her faith experience (p. 245) (**F**).

48. Some theories of development state that individuals will all pass through the theory's identified stages, while other theories assume that individuals have the capability to pass through all stages, but do not always do so (p. 246) (**T**).

49. All developmental theories are hierarchical, which means that later stages are better than earlier ones (p. 246) (**F**).

50. Predictable stages of cultural identity exist and effective counselors should examine their own cultural identity (pp. 246-247) (**T**).

INFOTRAC KEY WORDS: Developmental theories. Developmental issues. Child development. Adult development.

CHAPTER 10

ABNORMAL DEVELOPMENT, DIAGNOSIS, AND PSYCHOPHARMACOLOGY

Multiple Choice

1. In which of the following areas is the study of abnormal development *not* particularly needed (p. 253)?
   a. Agencies   b. Colleges   c. Schools   **d.** None of the above (it is needed in all)

2. Which of the following is *not* a reason for the counselors to study abnormal development, diagnosis, and/or psychopharmacology (pp. 254, 276)?
   a. Changes in federal law, such as requirements of PL94-142
   b. The increase in the number of individuals institutionalized in state mental hospitals
   c. So that counselors can have a common language with which to converse with the clinicians
   d. Because diagnosis can sometimes be helpful in creating treatment plans
   e. Because medications are helpful in treatment regimes

3. All but which of the following are some of the reasons how DSM-IV-TR can be helpful (p. 254)?
   a. It provides a common language for clinicians
   b. It offers a mechanism for understanding behaviors that deviate form the norm
   c. Classification offers one the ability to research which treatment strategies might be most helpful
   d. It provides a basis for differential treatment planning
   e. It provides a listing of which medications works best for different diagnoses

4. Which of the following represents the most recent thinking about biology, genetics, the environment, and mental illness (pp. 255-256)?
   a. A genetic predisposition probably exists for many forms of mental illness and even many less severe emotional problems
   b. There is a bidirectional interplay between genetics, biology, and environment
   c. The environment plays little, if any role in mental illness
   d. Psychotherapy can do little good for individuals with mental illness
   e. a and b
   f. c and d

5. Which represents Freud's "Structure of Personality"? (p. 257) (www)
   a. Id, ego, superego
   b. Oral, anal, phallic, latency, genital stages
   c. Defense mechanisms
   d. All of the above

6. According to Freud, this part of the personality represents the formation of morality and is influenced by the values of parents and society (pp. 257-258).
   a. Ego   **b.** Superego   c. Id   d. Libido

7. Irving receives erotic pleasure from having bowel movements. He is in which of Freud's stages (pp. 257-258)?
   a. Genital   b. Phallic   c. Oral   **d.** Anal   e. Latency

8. Which is the correct order of Freud's psychosexual stages of development (pp. 257-258)?
   a. Oral, anal, genital, phallic, latency
   b. Oral, anal, phallic, genital, latency
   c. Oral, anal, genital, latency, phallic
   d. Oral, anal, phallic, latency, genital

9. Sylvester enjoys playing with his own genitals. He is probably in which of Freud's stages (pp. 257-258)?
   a. Genital   **b.** Phallic   c. Oral   d. Anal   e. Latency

10. A child who has parents who are particularly strict around the anal stage may have children who (pp. 257-258):
  a. are passive and laissez-fair as adults
  b. become schizophrenic
  c. are irresponsible, messy, disorderly, and controlling of others
  d. are fastidious, compulsively clean, and fearful of dirt
  e. a and b
  f. c and d

11. The psychoanalytic stage of development that is crucial to the development of attachments, identification with gender roles, and the development of the superego is which of the following (pp. 257-258)?
  a. Genital **b.** Phallic c. Oral d. Anal e. Latency

12. The psychoanalytic stage of development in which we replace sexual energy with socialization is called the __________ stage (pp. 257-258).
  a. genital b. phallic c. oral d. anal **e.** latency

13. The Oedipus and Electra complex are (pp. 257-258):
  a. when we identify with the same-sex parent
  b. want to possess the opposite-sex parent
  c. want to eliminate the same-sex parent
  d. develop a sense of moral responsibility
  e. Two of the above
  f. Three of the above
  g. All of the above

14. Negative reinforcement is which of the following (p. 259)?
  a. The removal of a stimulus that leads to an increase in behavior
  b. The addition of a stimulus that leads to an increase in behavior
  c. The addition of an aversive stimulus that leads to a decrease in behavior
  d. The removal of a stimulus that leads to a decrease in behavior
  e. The ceasing of a behavior because it is not reinforced

15. The ceasing of a behavior because it is not reinforced is called (p. 259): (www)
  a. negative reinforcement
  b. operant reduction
  c. extinction
  c. extinction
  d. All of the above

16. The tendency for stimuli that are similar to a conditioned stimulus to take on the power of the conditioned stimulus is called (p. 260):
  a. positive reinforcement
  b. discrimination
  c. generalization
  d. spontaneous recovery
  e. None of the above

17. The tendency for responses to recur after they have been extinguished is called (p. 260):
  a. re-reinforcement
  b. generalization
  c. positive reinforcement
  d. reactivation
  e. spontaneous recovery

18. The most common kind of conditioning is generally considered to be which of the following (p. 259)?
  a. Operant b. Classical c. Modeling d. All are equally common

19. A client has trouble being spontaneous and does not feel good about him or herself. However, she feels a sense of community with her peer group. On which level of Maslow's hierarchy is she (p. 243)?
  a. Physiological
  b. Self-esteem
  c. Safety
  d. Self-actualization
  e. Love & belonging

19. Which of the following is *not* true about the learning theory perspective on personality development (p. 259-260)?
   a. A person is determined, by early reinforcement contingencies, to take on specific personality characteristics.
   b. Behaviors, cognitions, and the models that we view are continually reinforced by significant others and by cultural influences.
   c. Our behaviors will remain fairly constant unless we change the reinforcers in our environment.
   d. Reinforcement contingencies that lead to particular behaviors and ways of thinking are generally very complex, and can occur in very subtle ways.
   e. Abnormal development (or healthy development) is the result of the kinds of behaviors and cognitions that have been continually reinforced in our lives.
   f. By analyzing current reinforcement contingencies we can understand why an individual continues to exhibit his or her current behavioral and cognitive repertoire.
   g. All of the above are true.

21. Which is the correct order of Maslow's hierarchy (p. 262)?
   a. Physiological, self-esteem, safety, self-actualization, love and belonging
   b. Self-esteem, safety, self-actualization, love and belonging, physiological
   c. Physiological, safety, love and belong, self-esteem, self-actualization
   d. Safety, physiological, self-esteem, self-actualization, love and belonging
   e. Safety, physiological, self-esteem, love and belonging, self-actualization

22. Rogers believed in all but which of the following (pp. 261-262)?
   a. We all have a need to be loved
   b. We will act in ways to please others in order to receive love
   c. People will place conditions of worth on us in order to get us to act in certain ways
   d. Nongenuine living is necessary, at times, if we are to survive in a civilized world

23. In terms of personality development, Rogers believed which of the following (pp. 261-262))?
   a. People were born good and had a natural actualizing tendency
   b. Unconscious forces could thwart one's actualizing tendency
   c. Reinforcers in the environment had a major impact on personality formation
   d. Two of the above

24. Which of the following is *not* correctly matched (p. 269)?
   a. Axis I: Personality disorders and mental retardation
   b. Axis II: Clinical disorders and other conditions that may be a focus of clinical attention
   c. Axis III: General Medical conditions
   d. Axis IV: Psychosocial and Environmental Problems
   e. Axis V: Global Assessment of Functioning
   f. a and b
   g. d and e

26. Which of the following is a function of DSM-IV-TR (pp. 254, 265)? (www)
   a. It helps us understand the etiology of mental-health problems.
   b. It helps us in the diagnosis of mental-health problems.
   c. It is often used for insurance companies to assess claims for mental-health coverage.
   d. b and c
   e. All of the above

27. What is wrong with the following diagnosis (pp. 269-270)?

Axis I:	300.3: Obsessive-Compulsive Disorder
Axis II:	None
Axis III:	714.0: Rheumatoid Arthritis
Axis IV:	Job Loss
Axis V:	GAF = 60 (current); 70 (past year)

   a. Some of the diagnoses are on the wrong axes
   b. One cannot have a GAF score of "70"
   c. One cannot have a diagnosis of "none"
   d. Nothing is wrong with the above diagnoses

28. Referring to item 27. What does the GAF scores refer to (p. 270)?
   a. A score of "70" means there have been mild symptoms within the past year
   b. A score of "60" means there have been moderate symptoms recently
   c. A score of "60" means there have been mild symptoms within the past year
   d. A score of "70" means there have been moderate symptoms within the past year
   e. a and b
   f. c and d
   g. None of the above

29. Which of the following accurately lists how medications for the treatment of emotional disorders are generally categorized (p. 271)?
   a. Anxiety agents, antidepressants, hallucinogens, barbiturates,
   b. Stimulants, hallucinogens, barbiturates, common drugs, antianxiety
   c. Non-prescription pharmaceuticals, stimulants, barbiturates, antidepressants, antianxiety
   d. Antipsychotics, antimanics, antidepressants, antianxiety, stimulants

30. Antipsychotics are used for the treatment of all of the following except (p. 271):
   a. psychotic disorders
   b. bipolar disorders
   c. depression with psychotic features
   d. paranoid disorders
   e. delirium and dementia
   f. borderline personality disorder
   g. All of the above

31. One drug of choice for Bipolar Disorder is (p. 272): (www)
   a. Haldol b. Prozac c. Valium d. Welbutrin e. Lithium

32. SSRIs are (p. 272):
   a. a relatively new class of drugs to treat psychoses
   b. a relatively new class of drugs to treat anxiety
   c. a relatively new class of drugs to treat depression
   d. a relatively new class of drugs to treat personality disorders

33. Which of the following is not treated through the use of stimulants (p. 273)?
   a. Attention Deficit Disorder
   b. Narcolepsy
   c. Depression
   d. All of the above are used

34. Relative to diagnosis and multicultural counseling, which is *not* true (p. 274)?
   a. Some believe that the use of diagnosis is a way of legitimizing socially unacceptable behaviors and thus legally give others the right to oppress the culturally different
   b. Minorities may be misdiagnosed more frequently as the result of counselor bias
   c. DSM-IV-TR has a listing of 25 syndromes that are culture bound afflictions or illnesses which could be falsely mistaken for a diagnostic category
   d. DSM-IV-TR is a major step forward in helping clinicians deal with the problems of misdiagnosis and the culturally different client

35. Which of the following statements would R. D. Laing or Thomas Szasz most likely make (p. 275)?
   a. "Abnormal" behavior is a normal response to a situation
   b. There is much evidence to genetic and biological determinants of abnormal behavior
   c. Psychotic behavior represents repressed memories
   d. DSM-IV-TR represents a good attempt at explaining abnormal behavior

36. Which of the following is *not* true (p. 275)?
   a. Diagnosis is an objective process in which the person making the diagnosis is really not "in the shoes" of the person being diagnosed.
   b. Diagnosis tends to rob people of their uniqueness.
   c. Diagnosis can lead to a self-fulfilling prophecy for both the client and clinician (I think therefore I am)
   d. A diagnosis is not particularly useful in helping to decide on a specific psychotropic medication.
   e. Diagnosis leads to tunnel vision where the clinician attempts to "fit" all problems into the specific diagnostic category.

37. As a result of Donaldson v. O'Connor, (p. 276): (www)
    a. individuals in mental hospitals cannot be held against their will for extended periods of time
    b. psychiatrists must not be arbitrary in their use of medication
    c. If a client is in danger of harming another, the mental health practitioners must warn person who is in danger
    d. students cannot be labeled with a learning disability without appropriate testing

True or False

38. There is little evidence that mental illness is related biologically rooted (pp. 255-256) **(F)**.

39. There is little evidence that mental illness is genetically linked (pp. 255-256) **(F)**.

40. There is little evidence that mental illness is related to environmental conditions (pp. 255-256) **(F)**.

41. Probably, most diagnoses on Axis II of DSM-IV-TR have a basis in genetics (p. 256) **(T)**.

42. According to Freud, the child is born with an id, but not with an ego or superego **(T)** (p. 257).

43. The psychosexual stages affect the development of the structures of personality **(T)** (p. 257).

44. Ultimately, it is the ability to rid ourselves of our id that makes us a healthy person (p. 257) **(F)**.

45. Most learning theorists today believe that the child is born an empty slate, ready to reflect the world based on reinforcement contingencies (p. 259) **(F)**.

46. Recently, learning theorists have included a cognitive framework in their understanding of personality development (pp. 259-260) **(T)**.

47. Maslow stated that higher order needs can occur prior to lower order needs being fulfilled **(F)** (pp. 261-262).

48. According to Rogers, Maslow's hierarchy did not adequately explain the development of the person (pp. 261-262) **(F)**.

49. Rogers believed that the most important quality for the development of personality was the relationship between the child and his or her caretakers (pp. 261-262) **(T)**.

50. In reference to personality formation, it is common for mental health practitioners to find themselves in different "camps" (p. 263) **(F)**.

51. Axis III diagnostic categories are usually taken from the ICD-9-CM Codes (p. 268) **(T)**.

52. Antipsychotics were originally discovered in the early 1900s (p. 271) **(F.)**

53. The development of antipsychotics resulted in the release of hundreds of thousands of individuals from mental hospitals (p. 271) **(T)**.

54. It is nearly impossible to become addicted or overdose on antianxiety drugs like Librium (p. 273) **(F)**.

55. The newer antianxiety medications are much less addictive than their earlier counterparts (p. 273) **(T)**.

56. Cocaine was one of the first modern-day stimulants used to treat emotional disorders (p. 273) **(T)**.

57. Unfortunately, the ACA code of ethics does not address cultural differentness as it relates to the misuse of diagnosis (p. 274) **(F)**.

58. William Glasser believes that psychopathology is irresponsible behavior (p. 275) **(T)**.

INFOTRAC KEY WORDS: DSM-IV-TR. Psychopathology. Psychopharmacology.

CHAPTER 11

CAREER DEVELOPMENT: THE COUNSELOR AND THE WORLD OF WORK

Multiple Choice

1. The sequence of positions and/or jobs available to persons within an organization or business is called one's (p. 281):
   a. career b. occupation **c.** career path d. work

2. Career development is (p. 281):
   a. all of the psychological, sociological, educational, physical, economic, and other factors that shape one's career
   b. the consciousness that one has about his or her career-related which can be facilitated through self-examination
   c. the totality of work and life roles that a person takes on in life through which the individual expresses him- or herself
   d. All of the above

3. Leisure is (p. 281):
   a. a chosen activity, not necessarily pursued for money, that gives satisfaction to the individual
   b. time taken from required effort (e.g., job or occupation) in order to pursue self-chosen activities that express one's abilities and/or interests
   c. a chosen activity, pursued for money, that gives satisfaction to the individual
   d. Two of the above

4. An activity not necessarily pursued for money that gives satisfaction and fulfillment is (p. 281): (www)
   a. work b. job **c.** avocation D. career path

5. A relationship in which the focus is on the career development process to increase career awareness and decision making (p. 281):
   a. career development c. career path
   b. career Awareness **d.** career counseling

6. Time taken from a job to pursue self-chosen activities (p. 281):
   a. leisure b. avocation c. career awareness d. work

7. Career development is (p. 281): (www)
   a. the process of finding a job
   b. the shaping of our life roles
   c. the fulfillment of economic, social, and psychological needs for the individual
   d. All of the above

8. Which of the following is not part of the career development process of a person (p. 281)?
   a. The three-year-old who is trying to understand sex roles
   b. The thirteen-year-old who is comparing his abilities to others in his peer group
   c. The thirty-five-year-old who has taken on a new hobby
   d. The seventy-year-old who is about to retire
   e. Two of the above are not a part of the career development process
   f. None of the above (all are part of the process)

9. Work serves all of the following purposes except (p. 282):
   a. gratification of wants or needs
   b. feeling of competence
   c. social status
   d. potential friendships
   e. None of the above (All of the above serve a purpose for work)

10. Which theorist suggested that vocational guidance involved a three-step process which included knowing one self, knowing job characteristics, and making a match between the two (p. 283)?
   a. Super b. Holland c. Roe **d.** Parsons e. Ginzberg

11. Which act established the U.S. Employment Services (p. 283)?
   a. National Defense Education Act
   b. Civil Rights Act
   c. Wagner O'Day Act
   d. Community Mental Health Centers Act

12. ____________developed the first systematic approach to vocational guidance (p. 283).
   a. Jesse Davis **b.** Frank Parsons c Anna Reed d. Wagner O'Day

13. Which of the following individuals was *not* involved with the development of career guidance programs in the schools near the turn of the century (p. 283)?
   a. Jesse Davis B. Eli Weaver c. Anna Reed **d.** Ann Roe

14. Which theorist(s) was (were) the first to emphasize the concept of lifelong career development (p. 283)?
   a. Ginzberg
   b. Super
   c. Roe
   d. Holland
   e. Parsons
   f. a and b
   g. c and d
   h. d and e

15. The National Defense Education Act (NDEA) did which of the following (p. 283)?
   a. Stressed the importance of vocational rehabilitation
   b. Stressed the importance of career counseling for the military
   c. Stressed the importance of career guidance in the schools
   d. All of the above

16. Comprehensive models of career guidance of the 1960s and 1970s did all but which of the following (p. 284)?
   a. Focused on lifelong patterns of career development
   b. Assisted individuals in making choices that reflected their sense of self
   c. Suggested that career counseling was a three-step process of identification of personal qualities, identification of abilities, and matching the two
   d. Examined leisure and avocational activities when working with clients
   e. Viewed career development as a flexible and changeable process as compared to the rigid, irreversible process of earlier times
   f. Emphasized the individual, not the counselor, as the career decision-maker

17. ________ and ______ are two divisions of ACA committed to career development issues (p. 301).
   a. NCDA, NECA
   b. NCDA, ACES
   c. ACPA, NECA
   d. ACPA, ACES

18. Which theory states that the career choices we make our often out of our control (e.g., an economic depression) (p. 284)? (www)
   a. Self-efficacy theory
   b. Personality-based theory
   c. Developmental theory
   d. Decision-making theory
   e. Situational theory

19. Which theory states that the types of career choices we make in our lives are based on our beliefs about whether or not we can do certain behaviors (p. 284)?
   a. Self-efficacy theory
   b. Personality-based theory
   c. Developmental theory
   d. Decision-making theory
   e. Situational theory

20. Modern-day trait-and-factor theory assumes all but which of the following (p. 284)?
   a. Insight and knowledge of self is crucial to good matching
   b. Client counselor interaction is an important part of the process
   c. Individuals have unique traits which can be measured
   d. Awareness of unconscious factors is a crucial aspect of understanding self
   e. Occupations necessitate that individuals have certain traits if they are to be successful in that occupation

21. The trait-and-factor approach to career guidance assumes that (p 284):
   a. An individual's career interests will continue to change as she or he grows and develops
   b. Each individual is unique and has more traits than can be measured validly and reliably
   c. When an individual's personal characteristics are matched closely with job requirements, there is a higher probability for success
   d. An individual's traits are frequently influenced by situational factors which occur
   e. The matching of one's Holland personality codes to work codes is essential for effective career guidance

22. The Holland codes do which of the following (p. 269)?
   a. Matches personality type to job type
   b. Are helpful in understanding early parenting styles and how they relate to one's career choices
   c. Are codes that define types of job characteristics in the Occupational Outlook Handbook (OOH)
   d. Are used in understanding one's career development stage
   e. Two of the above

23. Which is *not* true of Hollands theory (pp. 285 - 288)?
   a. genetic and environmental influences leads people to develop a hierarchy of habitual or preferred methods for dealing with social and environmental tasks
   b. Numerous occupations can fit a personality type
   c. Lifespan issues are crucial in understanding the individual's career choices
   d. People express their personality through the types of career choices they make

24. Roe hypothesized that, relative to career choices, parents are either (p. 288):
   a. open or closed
   b. accepting or judgmental
   c. warm or cold
   d. disenfranchised or enmeshed

25. Which theorist emphasized the role of early parenting on career choice (p. 288)? (www)
   a. Super b. Holland c. Roe d. Parsons e. Ginzberg

26. Roe stated that __________ parents are indulgent with their children and demonstrative with their affection and have children who gravitate to the service, arts, or entertainment fields (p. 289).
   a. protective
   b. demanding
   c. loving
   d. rejecting
   e. neglecting
   f. casual

27. Roe stated that __________ parents ignore the child, give little attention, and have children who tend to develop science and outdoor interests (p. 289).
   a. protective
   b. demanding
   c. loving
   d. rejecting
   e. neglecting
   f. casual

28. Roe stated that __________ parents give emotional and physical attention to the child, but only after higher-priority issues in their own lives have been attended to and have children who tend to gravitate to technological occupations (p. 289).
   a. protective
   b. demanding
   c. loving
   d. rejecting
   e. neglecting
   f. casual

29. Which theorist views career development as a life long process in which we make choices based on our view of self (p. 289)?
   a. Super b. Holland c. Roe d. Parsons

30. Which is the correct order of Super's developmental stages (p. 290)?
   a. Exploration, Decline, Growth, Establishment, Maintenance
   b. Exploration, Growth, Establishment, Maintenance, Decline
   c. Growth, Exploration, Establishment, Maintenance, Decline
   d. Growth, Exploration, Maintenance, Establishment, Decline

31. Which of Super's stages involves stabilizing career choices and advancing in chosen fields (p. 290)?
a. Decline b. Exploration c. Growth **d.** Establishment e. Maintenance

32. Fifteen-year-old Lonnie is fantasizing about being a rap singer when he gets older and is comparing his singing ability to his peers. Fred is in which of Super's stages (p. 290)?
a. Decline **b.** Exploration c. Growth d. Establishment e. Maintenance

33. Jane is 35 years old and is advancing in her career as dentist. Jane is in which of Super's stages (p. 290)?
a. Decline b. Exploration c. Growth **d.** Establishment e. Maintenance

34. Four-year-old Hannah is excited about going to the firehouse for a field trip. Hannah is in which of Super's stages (p. 290)?
a. Decline b. Exploration **c.** Growth d. Establishment e. Maintenance

35. Cognitive development theories believe that career development is related to which of the following (p. 291)? (www)
a. Irrational or rational thinking
b. Situational factors that affect the way we think and ultimately our career choices
c. How individuals make meaning out of the world of work
d. All of the above

36. Which of the following is *not* a basic tenet of the cognitive development approaches to career development (p. 291)?
a. Cognitive development occurs in a series of predictable stages, which are the same for all people
b. People will differ in their rate of progression through the stages and some may become arrested in a stage.
c. Stage development is fixed and determined by early child rearing experiences and the kinds of messages we received as children
d. Higher stages are distinguished by more complex and more sophisticated ways of understanding the world
e. Sometimes, when faced with stressful situations, people may respond at lower stages.

37. Cognitive development theorists believe that the best manner in which to change a person's meaning making system is by (p. 291):
a. confronting the person's meaning-making system
b. using empathy and allowing the individual to find his or her own answers
c. exploring self-talk and such cognitive concepts as automatic thoughts
d. supporting and challenging the individuals meaning-making system

38. This source of occupational information has a nine-code classification with describes the use of data on the job, type of interactions with people at work, and the use of different types of things on the job (p. 277).
a. The Strong b. SIGI **c.** The DOT d. The DAT

39. This publication of the U.S. Department of Labor is a comprehensive classification system which describes 30,000 occupations (p. 2294).
a. Occupational Outlook Handbook
b. Dictionary of Occupational Titles
c. Guide for Occupational Exploration
d. General Aptitude Test Battery

40. Originally published in 1979, this occupational classification system is designed around 12 interest factors and offers detailed descriptions of about 2500 jobs (p. 294).
a. Occupational Outlook Handbook
b. Dictionary of Occupational Titles
c. Guide for Occupational Exploration
d. Government Survey of Occupational Trends

41. This publication of the U.S. Department of Labor gives information regarding the future demand for selected occupations; including facts regarding training requirements, wages, and employment conditions for these occupations (p. 295):
   a. Dictionary of Occupational Titles
   b. Occupational Outlook Handbook
   c. Guide for Occupational Exploration
   d. Government Survey of Occupational Trends

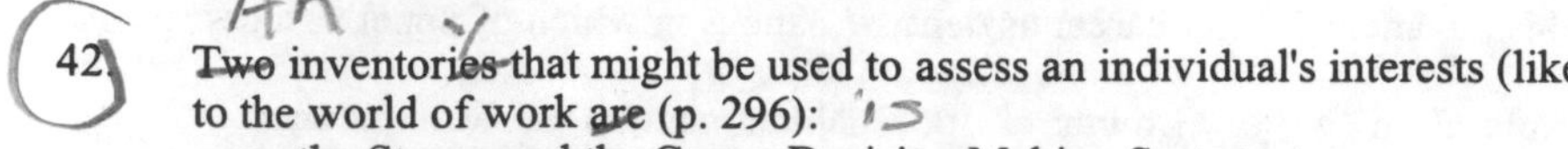

42. Two inventories that might be used to assess an individual's interests (likes and dislikes) as they relate to the world of work are (p. 296):
   a. the Strong and the Career Decision Making System
   b. SIGI and GIS
   c. the DOT and the OOH
   d. the DAT and GATB

43. Which of the following are aptitude tests which might be given to examine an individual's abilities as they relate to his or her career choices (p. 296)? (www)
   a. The Strong and the CDM
   b. SIGI and GIS
   c. The DOT and the OOH
   d. The DAT and GATB

44. Which of the following are examples of computer-generated career assessments that examine abilities, interests, values, and skills of the individual (p. 297)?
   a. The Strong and the CDM
   b. SIGI and GIS
   c. The DOT and the OOH
   d. The DAT and GATB

45. In reference to career development, the clinical interview (p. 298):
   a. is one of our most important counseling tools
   b. is less helpful as compared to the use of assessment instruments
   c. is our way of operationalizing career development theories
   d. Two of the above
   e. None of the above

46. McAuliffe's CPSS model of career development (p. 299):
   a. is an integrative model
   b. suggests that all counselors should examine the client's "context"
   c. suggests that all counselors should examine the clients phase or stage level
   d. suggests that all counselors should examine the client's personality style
   e. Two of the above
   f. Three of the above
   g. All of the above

47. McAuliffe's CPPS model of career development is an acronym for (p. 299):
   a. context, phase, stage, style
   b. career, personality, situation, self
   c. career, personality, stage, style
   d. career, personality, stage self-assessment

48. A client who is doing poorly in high school tells you that she would like to go to medical school. Your best response would be which of the following (p. 299)?
   a. Strongly discourage such an attempt.
   b. Encourage the client, noting that you know that he or she will succeed in whatever he or she chooses to do.
   c. Affirm the clients desire to go into the medical school, and point out the realities of what that would entail.
   d. Suggest career counseling in order to help the client understand she will never make it into medical school.

49. The developmentally mature counselor views career development as a(n) (p. 303):
   a. life-span process.
   b. as a process that might take a new direction as one goes through life.
   c. as process where one eventually discovers the correct field and happily remains in that career for the rest of his or her life.
   d. a and b
   e. a and c
   f. b and c

50. Relative to multicultural issues and career counseling, which of the following is *not* true (p. 300)?
   a. Cultural values and practices may make full access to the workplace more difficult for some minorities
   b. Whereas mainstream America has lived a life of upward mobility, some cultures and classes have not lived this dream and approach career development with different goals and aspirations
   c. The expression of self, and the development of self-concept through one's work is central to the career development process, regardless of cultural background
   d. The person-environment (personality-workplace) "fit," regardless of cultural background, is crucial for satisfaction at work
   e. Two of the above are not true
   f. None of the above (All are true)

51. Relative to multicultural issues and career counseling, which of the following is *not* true (p. 300)?
   a. The better the client understands his or her cultural identity development the easier it will be for the client to find a fit between self and environment.
   b. Discrimination in attaining jobs and at the workplace is a reality and needs to be addressed and acknowledge by career counselors.
   c. Discrimination and racism have resulted in some people having serious doubts about their ability to obtain jobs and be upwardly mobile
   d. Knowledge about the career development issues of specific minority groups is crucial to being an effective multicultural career counselor
   e. There are probably more differences within a cultural group than between cultural groups
   f. Assessment procedures, so prevalent in career counseling, may have inherent biases and may not have addressed how well they predict for minority groups and women.
   g. Two of the above are not true
   h. None of the above (All are true)

52. Which law(s) specifically prohibits discrimination against women and minorities in all aspects of employment (p. 303)?
   a. American with Disabilities Act
   b. PL94-142
   c. PL93-112
   d. Carl Perkins Act
   e. Title VII and Title IX
   f. Two of the above

53. Which law assures access to vocational rehabilitation services for adults if they meet certain conditions (p. 302)?
   a. American with Disabilities Act
   b. PL94-142
   c. Rehabilitation Act of 1973
   d. Title VII and Title IX

54. Which law authorized grants for the expansion of career guidance programs for students and others who had vocational education needs (p. 302)? (www)
   a. American with Disabilities Act
   b. PL94-142
   c. PL93-112
   d. Carl Perkins Act
   e. Title VII and Title IX

55. Which law assures that qualified individuals with disabilities cannot be discriminated against in a number of job-related areas (p. 302)?
   a. American with Disabilities Act
   b. PL94-142
   c. Rehabilitation Act of 1973
   d. Carl Perkins Act
   e. Title VII and Title IX

need answer

A person's main interests lie in building. The most closely matched code is: a) artistic (b) realistic c) enterprising d) investigative

True or False

56. Roe believed that early child-rearing practices in conjunction with genetics, interests, abilities, and other factors lead one to choose an occupation in one of eight areas (pp. 288-289) **(T)**.

57. Holland believed that career development is an ongoing, continuous, and orderly process starting in early childhood and ending with death (pp. 285-288)**(F)**.

58. Super believed that one's self-concept is both a function of and result of one's career development process (p. 290) **(T)**.

59. John Holland believes that regardless of our ability, we can fit into a number of work environments based on our personality (p. 285-288) **(T)**.

60. On Holland's hexagon, codes directly across from one another are more similar than those next to one another (p. 285) **(F)**.

61. Cognitive developmental theorists can apply their basic concepts using many developmental theories (p. 291) **(T)**.

62. Theories of career development vary so much that it is unusual to find a counselor integrating the various approaches (p. 192) **(F)**.

63. The Occupational Outlook Handbook examines approximately 10,000 jobs (p. 295) **(F)**.

64. The Career Assessment Inventory and The Career Decision-Making System are two types of Interest Inventories (p. 296) **(T)**.

65. Personality assessment, is not recommended when doing career counseling as it is not directly related to one's career choices as are interest inventories (p. 297) **(F)**.

66. Aptitude tests allow an individual to examine whether or not occupational preferences match the individual's ability (p. 297) **(T)**.

67. Due to copyright restrictions, it is not possible to download interest and ability tests directly off of the Internet (p. 298) **(F)**.

68. PL93-112 requires colleges to provide career services to people with disabilities (p. 301) **(T)**.

69. The School-to-Work Opportunities Act provides incentives to help schools and community colleges develop programs that integrate academic learning with on the job experiences (p. 303) **(T)**.

70. Because of their diverse views on the career development process, few career development counselors integrate different career development models (p. 299) **(F)**.

(Questions 71-81) Matching (pp. 280-281)

71. A group of similar positions in a single institution or organization (**c**). — a. avocation

72. A term used to describe a series of positions in a specialized work area usually connoting possibilities for advancement (**d**). — b. leisure

73. The total constellation of psychological, educational physical, economic, and chance factors that combine to shape the career of a person over the life span (**e**). — c. job

74. Time free from required effort for the free use of abilities and pursuits of interests (**b**). — d. career path

75. A group of similar jobs found in different industries or organizations (**g**). — e. career development

76. An activity pursued systematically and consecutively for its own sake with an objective other than monetary gain (**a**). — f. career awareness

77. The inventory of knowledge, values preferences, and self-concepts that an individual draws on in the course of making career-related choices (**f**). — g. occupation

78. An individual or group counseling relationship in which the focus is on the career development process (**i**). — h. work

79. The totality of occupations and roles that a person takes on in life through which the individual expresses his or her self (**k**). — i. career counseling

80. A program designed by counselors which offers information concerning any aspects of career development and facilitates career awareness for individuals (**j**). — j. career guidance

81. Effort expended in pursuit of a job, occupation, or avocation in order to produce or accomplish something (**h**). — k. Career

(Questions 82-87) Matching (p. 286)
Match the following descriptions with the appropriate Holland personality types:

82.	People who are concrete, like to work with data, and prefer routine problem solving. They prefer clerical tasks and tend to be neat, follow instructions, and look for social approval (**f**).	a. Artistic
83.	People who are concerned for others, nurturing, introspective, responsible, like social situations, and are verbally skilled (**e**).	b. Enterprising
84.	People who like to investigate, think abstractly, do problem solving, but who avoid social situations and tend to be introverted (**d**).	c. Realistic
85.	People who are persuasive, self confident, like to lead, and see themselves as stable, sociable, adventurous and bold (**b**).	d. Investigative
86.	People who are practical, robust, have good physical skills, like the outdoors, and who avoid social situations, intellectual pursuits, and artistic endeavors (**c**).	e. Social
87.	People who express themselves through creativity and imagination, like unstructured activities, and tend to be sensitive, introspective, and independent (**a**).	f. Conventional

(Questions 88-96) Matching Questions (pp. 284-294)

88.	___Self-Efficacy Theory (**d**)	a. Matching personality characteristics with career choices
89.	___Social Learning Theory (**f**)	b. Choices are out of our control
90.	___Decision Making Theory (**h**)	c. How individuals make meaning out of the world of work
91.	___Situational Theories (**b**)	d. Choices made based on beliefs about abilities
92.	___Trait-and-Factor Theory (**a**)	e. People express their personality through the career choices that they make
93.	___Holland's Personality Theory of Occupational Choice (**e**)	f. Choose career based on learned experience
94.	___Super's Lifespan Development Theory (**g**)	g. Called a developmental self concept theory
95.	___Cognitive Development Theories (**c**)	h. Make career choices based on self understanding
96.	___Psychodynamic Theory (**i**)	i. Career choice based on early parenting

INFOTRAC KEY WORDS: Career development theory. Computers and career assessment.Americans with Disability Act.

CHAPTER 12

TESTING AND ASSESSMENT

Multiple Choice

1. Which is *not* true about testing (p. 307)?
   a. Testing helps clients understand their abilities and their personality
   b. Testing can help in treatment planning
   c. Testing is often used in research and evaluation
   d. Testing can be helpful in diagnosis
   e. Testing is one aspect of assessment
   f. None of the above (testing does all of the above)

2. Which of the following would *not* be a use of tests for clients of a counselor (p. 307)?
   a. To assist clients in finding satisfactory employment
   b. To help identify learning disability of students
   c. To assist in the proper diagnosis of clients
   d. To assist in the proper treatment of clients
   e. None of the above (all are important uses)

3. Which of the following examined individual differences–a concept crucial to the beginning of the testing movement (p. 308)?
   a. Darwin b. Wundt c. Fechner d. Two of the above **e.** All of them

4. Which of the following was one of the first tests of individual intelligence (p. 308)?
   a. The Wechsler Intelligence Scale for Children
   b. The Cognitive Ability Test
   c. The Iowa Test of Basic Skills
   d. The Stanford-Binet

5. Which of the following did not affect the spread of assessment instruments at the beginning of the 20th century (p. 308)?
   a. The popularity of psychoanalysis
   b. Advances in the treatment of mental health
   c. The vocational guidance movement
   d. World War I

6. Achievement testing includes all but which of the following (p. 309)? (www)
   a. Survey battery tests
   b. Diagnostic tests
   c. Readiness tests
   d. Individual intelligence tests

7. Aptitude testing includes all but which of the following (p. 310)?
   a. Cognitive ability tests
   b. Individual intelligence tests
   c. Special aptitude tests
   d. Multiple aptitude tests
   e. Achievement tests

8. Examples of two types of achievements tests include which of the following (p. 309)?
   a. WISC-II and the ASVAB
   b. ASVAB and GATB
   c. Iowa Test of Basic Skills and Stanford
   d. SATs and GREs

9. Which of the following are examples of two types of cognitive ability tests (p. 311)?
   a. WISC-II and the ASVAB
   b. ASVAB and GATB
   c. Iowa Test of Basic Skills and Stanford
   d. SATs and GREs

10. Which of the following are examples of two types of multiple aptitude tests (p. 311)?
    a. WISC-II and the ASVAB
    b. ASVAB and GATB
    c. Iowa Test of Basic Skills and Stanford
    d. SATs and GREs

11. Personality assessment measures all but which of the following (p. 312)?
   a. Temperament   d. Likes and dislikes   g. Two of the above
   b. Attitudes   e. Motivation   h. Three of the above
   c. Values   f. Adjustment   **i.** All are measured by personality assessment

12. The MMPI-II and the Myers-Briggs are two (p. 312):
   a. projective tests   **c.** objective tests of personality
   b. interest inventories   d. None of the above

13. How many interest inventories, on average, are given each year (p. 313)?
   a. 10,000   b. 1,000,000   c. 50,000   **d.** 3,000,000

14. Which of the following is not true about informal assessment procedures (p. 313)?
   a. They are less valid than formal assessment procedures
   b. They are relatively easy to use
   c. They examine a "slice" a an individual's behavior
   d. They are generally produced by national publishing companies

15. Tests of Interest Inventories and Objective Personality Measures generally can be considered (p. 312):
   a. tests in the affective domain   c. tests in the cognitive domain
   b. non-standardized tests   d. None of the above
   c. informal impressionistic tests

16. Which of the following is not a type of informal assessment procedure (pp. 313-314)?
   a. Structured interviews   d. Journals
   b. Journals   e. Situational tests
   c. Cumulative records   **f.** Projective tests

17. I am interested in exploring empathic responses of a specific counselor trainee. I therefore view all of this trainee's counseling sessions with a client and rate the counselor's responses. This is an example of (p. 314):
   a. sociometric measure   **c.** event sampling
   b. time sampling   d. semantic ratings

18. A highly trained specialist examines a client's responses to a series of ink blots. Which of the following was the client given (p. 312)? (www)
   a. An interest inventory   d. An achievement test
   b. An objective personality test   **e.** A projective test
   c. An ability test

19. Steve is assessed by his special education, teacher by a test she created, to see if he has reached agreed upon learning goals. Steve was given which of the following (p. 314)?
   a. Standardized, norm-referenced test   c. Informal, norm-referenced test
   b. Standardized, criterion-referenced test   **d.** Informal, criterion-referenced test

20. In administering an individual intelligence test to a number of clients I give it the same way, every time. In analyzing the results, I compare my clients' scores to those of their peer groups. This is an example of which of the following (p. 314)?
   a. Standardized, norm-referenced test   c. Informal, norm-referenced test
   b. Standardized, criterion-referenced test   d. Informal, criterion-referenced test

21. Poorva takes the national counselor exam. This test is likely which of the following (p. 314)?
   a. Standardized, norm-referenced test   c. Informal, norm-referenced test
   b. Standardized, criterion-referenced test   d. Informal, criterion-referenced test

(Questions 22-26) Identifying rating scales (pp. 314-314).
Place the appropriate "letter" that corresponds to the rating scales below

"A" = behavior checklist	"D" = numerical scale
"B" = sociometric measure	"E" = rank order
"C" = Likert scale	"F" = semantic differential

22. ____ Pick the item that best describes you: **(D)**
    1) very outgoing and social
    2) moderately outgoing and social
    3) slightly outgoing
    4) somewhat withdrawn
    5) very much withdrawn

23. ____ Rate how much you liked the book. **(C)**

    1________2________3________4________5
    not at all   a moderate amount   a lot

24. ____ Place an "X" next to the item that best describes you: **(A)**
    ___extroverted ___shy ___anxious
    ___happy ___introverted ___nurturing

25. ____ Place a 1 next to the type of therapy you think is most effective, a 2 next to the one you think is second most effective, and so forth, with a 5, representing the type of therapy you think is least effective. **(E)**
    ___Psychoanalytic___Humanistic___Behavioral___Transpersonal___Cognitive

26. ____ Place a mark on the line that best represents the relative strengths of your attributes as listed below. **(F)**
    introverted____extroverted
    happy____sad

27. Norm-referenced testing does all but which of the following (p. 314)?
    a. Allows an individual to compare him or herself to others
    b. Offers a way of understanding the subjective experience of the examinee
    c. Allows examinees to compare their results to one another
    d. Allows an individual to compare his or her results on two different tests

28. Talesha is given a test to measure preset learning goals, and her scores are later compared to a national sample. She was given which of the following (p. 314)? (www)
    a. Standardized, norm-referenced test
    b. Standardized, criterion-referenced test
    c. Informal, norm-referenced test
    d. Informal, criterion-referenced test

29. Jo, who is a slow learner, receives a score of 52 on a standardized achievement test. What can you say about this score (p. 315)?
    a. That she has done poorly
    b. That she has done well
    c. That she should not have been given an achievement test because she is probably learning disabled
    d. Nothing, unless you know something about the norm group scores

30. Which is not a measure of central tendency (p. 316)?
    a. The range b. The mean c. The median d. The mode

31. Which is not correctly matched (p. 316)?
    a. Mean = the average of all the scores
    b. Median = the middle score
    c. Mode = the most extreme score
    d. None of the above (All are correct)

32. Which of the following is not a measure of variability (p. 317)?
   a. The standard deviation
   b. The standard error of measurement
   c. The range
   d. The semi-interquartile range

33. Jill Jacobs receives a grade equivalent score of 10.6 on a national reading test. She is in the ninth grade. Which statement is *most* true about Jill (p. 320)?
   a. Her reading ability is equal to students at the 10th grade level.
   b. Based on the above score, no conclusions can be drawn.
   c. Jill is doing better than the average student in her grade level.
   d. Jill is doing worse than the average student in her grade level.
   e. Two of the above

34. A test has a mean of 40 and a standard deviation of 10 and is normally distributed. What percentage of people score between a 30 and 40 (p. 318)? (www)
   a. 2   b. 34   c. 68   d. 96

35. Khalil obtained a score of 590 on the S.A.T.'s (M=500, SD=100) and a score of 87 on the WISC-II. (M=100, SD=15). On which test did he do better (p. 319)?
   a. WISC-II
   b. SAT
   c. He performed equally well on both tests

36. Which of the following is not a derived score (p. 320)?
   a. Percentiles
   b. T-scores
   c. Correlation coefficients
   d. Grade equivalents
   e. SAT/GRE type scores
   f. Stanines
   g. Idiosyncratic publisher-derived scores

37. A derived score that ranges from 1 to 9 and is generally used with achievement tests is called a(n) (p. 320):
   a. SAT/GRE type score
   b. T-score
   c. stanine
   d. Idiosyncratic publisher-derived score

38. A derived score that has a mean of 500 and a standard deviation of 100 and is considered a cognitive ability test is a(n) (p. 320):
   a. SAT/GRE type score
   b. T-score
   c. Stanine
   d. Idiosyncratic publisher-derived score

39. A derived score that has a mean of 50 and a standard deviation of 10 and generally used with personality tests is a(n) (p. 320):
   a. SAT/GRE type score
   b. T-score
   c. Stanine
   d. Idiosyncratic publisher-derived score

40. Which is the strongest correlation (p. 320)?
   a. r = 0   b. r = + .90   c. r = -.99   d. r = +1.4

41. Two types of criterion-related validity are (p. 322):
   a. construct and predictive
   b. content and construct
   c. concurrent and predictive
   d. concurrent and construct

42. Test validity shows that (p. 321): (www)
   a. a test is measuring what is purports to measure
   b. that a test is fair in the manner it is given
   c. that a test measures scores in an accurate fashion
   d. All of the above

43. Many testing instruments are used to make a determination about future behavior. This is an example of which of the following (p. 322)?
   a. Predictive validity
   b. Practicality.
   c. A situational contextual measure
   d. Tests-retest reliability
   e. Future diagnostic ability

44. Test reliability shows that (p. 322):
   a. a test is measuring what is purports to measure
   b. that a test is fair in the manner it is given
   c. that a test measures scores in an accurate fashion
   d. All of the above

45. Which of the following concepts should be taken into account when testing (pp. 321-324)?
   a. the "wisdom" of the examiner
   b. validity and reliability
   c. the practicality of the test
   d. social/cultural issues
   e. Two of the above
   f. Three of the above
   g. all of the above

46. Which of the following is *not* important in using a test (pp. 316, 321-324)?
   a. Reliability and validity
   b. Practicality
   c. The norm group
   d. None of the above (all are important)

47. A schools system decides not to use a test because it is too costly and takes to long to administer. This is an issue of (p. 324):
   a. reliability
   b. validity
   c. practicality
   d. All of the above

48. The case that asserted that tests used for hiring and advancement at work must show that they can predict job performance for all groups is which of the following (p. 324)?
   a. Donaldson v. O'Connor
   b. Griggs v. Duke Power
   c. Miller v. Pallett
   d. Orange v. Gannett

49. Which of the following is not a good source to find information about tests (p. 325)? (www)
   a. The Internet
   b. Experts in the field
   c. Magazines that offer tests to take
   d. Books on testing
   d. Buros Mental Measurement Yearbook
   e. Tests in Print
   f. Journals in the field
   g. Publisher resources manuals

50. Which of the following is *not* correctly matched (p. 328)?
   a. A level A examiner should have a minimum of a master's degree, an overview course in testing, and specific course work in specialized testing,
   b. A level B examiner should have a master's degree in counseling or a related degree, and an overview course in testing.
   a. Level C examiner should be a responsible non-psychologist
   d. a and b are incorrect
   e. b and c are incorrect
   f. a and c are incorrect

51. Which of the following is the correct definition of informed consent (p. 328)?
   a. The understanding on the part of the counselor that she or he has to inform on any severe misconduct exhibited by his or her colleagues
   b. The client knowing about the nature tests that he or she will take and giving permission for testing
   c. The right of an administrator to be informed about the client's treatment
   d. All of the above.

52. Which of the following concepts should be taken into account when testing an individual (pp. 321-324, 329)?
   a. The "wisdom" of the examiner
   b. Validity and reliability
   c. Practicality
   d. Social/cultural issues
   e. All of the above

53. When writing test reports, which of the following *should be* done(p. 325)?
   a. Use plenty of psychological jargon
   b. Focus on the test and down play the person
   c. Focus on the person and de-emphasize the test results
   d. Take a position about the person who is being tested
   e. Be poorly organized or use poor writing skills

54. ACAs multicultural assessment standards do all but which of the following (p. 327)?
   a. Helps counselors and others understand the cultural bias inherent in tests
   b. Helps counselors understand that any test that has bias, should not be used
   c. Helps counselors know what do with tests results when a test *does not* predict well for minorities
   d. None of the above

55. Relative to assessment, the Buckley Amendment and the Freedom of Information Act do which of the following (p. 329)?
   a. Stresses the importance of informed consent when testing
   b. Assure the right of an individual to their tests results
   c. Assure the right to be tested for children who have a suspected disability
   d. Protect counselors from being sued for invasion of privacy while testing

56. Which is the current acronym of the ACA division that focuses on assessment (p. 329)?
   a. AMED **b.** AAC c. AHEAD d. ATC

57. Which law assures the right of individuals with disabilities to have access to vocational assessment (p. 330)?
   a. PL94-142 c. American with Disabilities Act
   b. Carl Perkins Act d. Civil Rights Acts of 1964 and its amendments

58. Which law asserts that accommodations must be made for individuals with disabilities who are taking tests for employment when the test is relevant to obtaining a job (p. 330)?
   a. PL94-142 **c.** American with Disabilities Act
   b. Carl Perkins Act d. Civil Rights Acts of 1964 and its amendments

59. A six-year old child is given a test, at the schools expense, to determine if the child has a learning disability in math. The child then is referred to a math specialist for tutoring, for one-hour a week, three times a week. This scenario reflects which of the following laws (p. 329)? (www)
   a. The American for Disabilities Act
   b. The Buckley Amendment
   c. The Freedom of Information Act
   d. Public Law 94-142 (PL94-142)

60. The law that asserts that tests used for hiring and advancement must be valid for the job in question is (p. 330):
   a. PL94-142 c. American with Disabilities Act
   b. Carl Perkins Act **d.** Civil Rights Acts of 1964 and its amendments

Questions (61-69) Matching

In determining the accuracy and relevancy of the National Counselor Exam, the creators of the test attempted to determine its reliability and validity. In the space provided, match the kind of reliability or validity (pp. 321-324).

61. ___They readministered the test one week later to a random sample of counselors (**A**).

62. ___They created two forms of the test and found the correlation coefficient (**H**).

63. ___They asked nationally known experts in counseling to submit sample items (**B**).

64. ___They took a sample of individuals who *very recently* received their master's degree and correlated graduate GPA with test scores (**E**).

65. ___They completed a statistical item analysis of the test results examining the mean of all possible split-half reliabilities (**C**).

66. ___They correlated one-half of the test items with the other half of the test items (**I**).

67. ___They correlated test scores from a sample of recent graduates with supervisor ratings of counselors' ability two years later (**G**).

68. ___They named the test "The National Certification Exam for Counselors" to reflect the nature of the test (**D**).

69. In creating the test they *hypothesized* that students with a master's degree in counseling would do significantly better than students with a master's degree in psychology. The results should support their theoretical assumptions about the test (**F**).

A. Test-retest reliability

B. Content validity

C. Coefficient alpha reliability (internal consistency)

D. Face validity

E. Concurrent validity

F. Construct validity

G. Predictive validity

H. Parallel forms reliability (alternate forms)

I. Odd-even reliability (split-half)

True or False

70. The Chinese used testing as far back as 2200 B.C.E. as a measure of physical prowess (p. 308) (**F**).

71. In the late 1800's, the French Department of Education hired Alfred Binet to develop an intelligence scale to identify those who could function in a classroom from those who could not (p. 308) (**T**).

72. Advances in statistics led to great changes in tests during the 1940s and 1950s (p. 309) (**T**).

73. The use of computers made statistical analysis of tests much easier (p. 309) (**T**).

74. Achievement testing measures what you have learned, aptitude testing measures what you're capable of learning (p. 309) (**T**).

75. The differences between achievement testing and aptitude testing is usually considerable (p. 312) (**F**).

76. Generally, assessment of personality is easier than assessment of ability (p. 312) (**F**).

77. Interest inventories are generally used for career counseling because of their strength in showing abilities of an individual (p. 312) (**F**).

78. If Leona scored a 95 on a test, she has done quite well (p. 315) (**F**).

79. The mean, median, and mode are types of measures of variability (p. 316) **(F)**.

80. Measures of variability tell you how much scores vary (p. 317) **(T)**.

81. The area between +1 and -1 standard deviations on a normal curve would include approximately 84% of the population (p. 318) **(F)**.

82. A student received a score on a norm-referenced standardized test that was two standard deviations below the mean. This person scored better than approximately 16% of his or her norm group (p. 318) **(F)**.

83. On a normally distributed curve, raw scores may become meaningful if you know the standard deviation and mean of the group (p. 319) **(T)**

84. You are more likely to find stanines used with personality assessment, DIQ's with achievement testing, and percentiles with intelligence testing (p. 320) **(F)**.

85. Though the common usages of DIQ's, percentiles, stanines, T-scores, and Grade Equivalents imply a different type of test they all measure the relative position of an individual as compared to the norm group (p. 320) **(T)**.

86. On a normally distributed curve, 50% of people would score below the mean (p. 300) **(T)**.

87. Validity tells you whether or not test scores are consistent (if examines were to take the test again, would they score about the same (pp. 321-322) **(F)**.

88. Reliability is to Consistency as Validity is to Content. (pp. 322-324) **(T)**.

89. Reliability tells you whether or not the test's content is adequate. **(F)** (pp. 322-323)

90. Cultural fairness refers to the concept that in the development, administration and interpretation of an assessment instrument, cross-cultural issues are taken into account. (p. 324) **(T)**.

91. One cannot eliminate all bias in tests (p. 324) **(T)**.

92. In reference to bias in testing, it is important to show that a test is not only predictive for the whole group, but predictive for subgroups (e.g., minorities) (p. 324).**(T)**.

93. Individuals should be informed about the purpose and nature of testing *before* a test is given (p. 324) **(T)**.

94. All tests invade one's privacy (p. 324) **(T)**.

95. Counselors can give all types of tests except for tests that need specialized training. In addition, if this training is obtained, they can also give these tests **(T)** (p. 328)

96. Parents have a right to their children's educational records, including test records. This is guaranteed through the Buckley amendment (p. 329) **(T)**.

97. Generally, one should be more concerned about patterns that emerge from a number of assessment procedures than scores on one particular test (p. 329) **(T)**.

Matching (Questions 98-107). Match the type of test with the brief definitions listed below (pp. 309-313).

___98. Temperament, or typical and/or habitual behaviors. Tests in the affective realm (**j**).	A) Achievement Test
___99. This paper and pencil test is used to predict behavior and generally measures verbal and quantitative skills (**h**).	B) Survey Battery Achievement Test
___100. Unstructured responses (**d**).	C) Diagnostic Test
___101. What a person is *capable of learning* (**f**).	D) Projective Test
___102. A test that can zero in on specific problem areas. problems (**c**).	E) Readiness Test
___103. Usually measuring educational achievement, this test examines whether a person is prepared to move on to the next level (**e**).	F) Aptitude Test
___104. What a person *has learned* (**a**).	G) Multiple Aptitude Test
___105. A number of homogenous segments of ability placed together in one test (**g**).	H) Cognitive Ability Test
___106. Measurement of a number of distinct cognitive abilities that yield one score (**i**).	I) Individual Intelligence Test
___107. This test measures a broad range of information that is generally learned in school (**b**).	J) Personality Test

INFOTRAC KEY WORDS: Ability testing. Personality testing. Achievement testing Aptitude testing. Projective testing. Intelligence and IQ.

CHAPTER 13

RESEARCH, PROGRAM EVALUATION AND APPRAISAL

Multiple Choice

1. Research in which there is an assumption that there is an objective reality in which questions can be formulated and scientific method used to measure behaviors is called (p. 335): (www)
   a. Statistics
   b. External validation
   c. Internal validation
   d. Quantitative research
   e. Qualitative research

2. Research in which there is an assumption that human behavior can only be understood within a social context and that one can make sense of an event or another culture by immersing oneself in that event or culture is called (p. 335):
   a. Statistics
   b. External validation
   c. Internal validation
   d. Quantitative research
   e. Qualitative research

3. Which of the following is an electronic search of abstracts (p. 336)?
   a. ERIC
   b. PsychINFO
   c. Counseling today
   d. Psychology today
   e. a and b
   f. b and c
   g. a and c

4. The ___________ places research into its historical context, discusses the issue at hand, and offers research questions, statements, and/or hypotheses (p. 336):
   a. Literature review
   b. Scope of the problem
   c. Statement of the problem
   d. Research design

5. The _____________ is manipulated to determine its effect on the ___________ (P. 337)
   a. Independent variable, dependent variable
   b. Independent variable, outcome measure
   c. Dependent variable, independent variable
   d. Dependent variable, outcome measure
   e. a and b
   f. b and c

6. I randomly assign subjects to one group that receives counseling skills training and another group that receives a lecture on the importance of counseling. I then compare the two groups on their ability to make empathic responses. What kind of research design is this (p. 337)?
   a. True experimental research
   b. Quasi-experimental research
   c. Single-subject design
   d. Causal-comparative research
   e. Survey research
   f. Correlational research

7. In reporting the results of a true experimental study, the researcher states that the results were significant and a function of the treatment given. This means that (p. 338):
   a. you have proven your hypothesis
   b. there is a very high probability that the results are a result of chance factors
   c. there is very low probability that your results are from treatment effects
   d. Two of the above
   e. All of the above

8. When a researcher comes to false conclusions about their study as a result of uncontrolled factors, it is called (p. 341): (www)
   a. threats to the hypothesis
   b. threats to the dependent variable
   c. threats to the independent variable
   d. threats to external validity
   e. threats to internal validity

9. I randomly assign one of three kinds of training in multicultural counseling to three counselor education programs, and then I measure the ability of students in each program to work with clients of color. What kind of research design is this (p. 340)?
   a. True experimental research
   b. Quasi-experimental research
   c. Single-subject design
   d. Causal-comparative research
   e. Survey research
   f. Correlational research

10. I have a subject learn relaxation methods and then measure their anxiety level. I do this a number of times a week and measure changes in baseline. What kind of research design is this (p. 340)? (www)
   a. True experimental research
   b. Quasi-experimental research
   c. Single-subject design
   d. Causal-comparative research
   e. Survey research
   f. Correlational research

11. I ask graduate students in counseling to take a number of instruments that measure dogmatism and internal locus of control. I also ask them to respond empathically to videotaped role-play clients and obtain a measure of their ability to be empathic. I then examine the relationship among dogmatism, internal locus of control, and empathy. What kind of research design is this (p. 341)?
   a. True experimental research
   b. Quasi-experimental research
   c. Single-subject design
   d. Causal-comparative research
   e. Survey research
   f. Correlational research

12. A study in which the relationship between a variable in the present and a variable in the future is examined is called which of the following (p. 3343)?
   a. True experimental research
   b. Quasi-experimental research
   c. Simple correlational study
   d. Causal-comparative research
   e. Survey research
   f. Predictive correlational study

13. I develop an instrument to assess the frequency of rate of counselors attendance in their own therapy. I send it to a random sample of 2,000 ACA members. What kind of research design is this (p. 343)?
   a. True experimental research
   b. Quasi-experimental research
   c. Single-subject design
   d. Causal-comparative research
   e. Survey research
   f. Correlational research

14. I compare differences in scores on the National Counselor Certification exam of students from five counselor education programs. What kind of research design is this (p. 345)? (www)
   a. True experimental research
   b. Quasi-experimental research
   c. Single-subject design
   d. Causal-comparative research
   e. Survey research
   f. Correlational research

15. Which of the following show(s) a causal relationship (p. 340)?
   a. Predictive correlational study
   b. Quasi-experimental research
   c. Simple correlational study
   d. Survey research
   e. Causal-comparative research

16. Which of the following show(s) a causal relationship (p. 337)?
   a. True experimental research
   b. Quasi-experimental research
   c. Single-subject design
   d. Simple correlational research
   e. Survey research

17. The degree to which extraneous variables have been accounted for is called which of the following (p. 341)?
   a. External validity
   b. Internal validity
   c. Reliability
   d. Test validity
   e. All of the above

18. The degree to which your results can be generalized and applied to a larger population is called which of the following (p. 352):
   a. External validity
   b. Internal validity
   c. Reliability
   d. Test validity
   e. All of the above

19. All but which of the following are examples of descriptive statistics (p. 348)?
   a. Measures of central tendency
   b. Measures of variability
   c. Derived scores (e.g., percentiles, T-scores)
   d. correlation coefficient
   e. All of the above are types of descriptive statistics

20. All but which of the following are examples of inferential statistics (p. 348)?
   a. Measures of variability
   b. Analysis of Variance (ANOVA)
   c. Multivariate Analysis of Variance (MANOVA)
   d. Chi square
   e. All of the above are types of inferential statistics

21. McMillan and Schumacher (2001) suggest that the degree to which a research design can represent objective reality is a mark that the study has good (p. 350):
   a. Validity
   b. Internality
   c. Reliability
   c. Probability
   d. All of the above

22. Deductive, reductionistic methods are used by (p. 346):
   a. qualititative researchers
   b. quantitative researchers
   c. all researchers

25. Another name for ethnographic research, is (p. 346): (www)
   a. the case study method
   b. observation
   c. Qualitative research
   d. cultural anthropology

26. Ethnographic research is (p. 346):
   a. a systematic analysis of the historical artifacts of a culture
   b. the understanding of an event or events of a culture from within the cultural context
   c. the observation of a culture in a nonengaged manner
   d. All of the above

27. Which of the following is generally not done in ethnographic research (pp. 346-348)?
   a. Observation
   b. Interviews
   c. Documents and artifact collection
   d. Extensive historical research

28. Which of the following is not stressed as a "issue of quality" in qualitative research (p. 328)?
   a. Ability to record information accurately
   b. The role of and the experience of the field researcher.
   c. Conducting a logical analysis of the information gathered
   d. The ability of the researcher to seek differing perspectives
   e. Conducting a thorough statistical analysis of the data

29. In understanding a culture, which of the following do ethnographers *not* do (pp. 346-348)?
   a. Collect personal documents
   b. Collect official documents
   c. Collect objects that hold symbolic meaning
   d. Conduct interviews
   e. None of the above (all are done by an ethnographer)

30. Historical research relies on all but which of the following (p. 348)?
   a. Participant observation
   b. Oral histories
   c. Documents
   d. Relics

31. Which of the following would not be done in historical research (p. 348)?
   c. Using primary sources over secondary sources
   b. Immersing oneself in the culture and interviewing large numbers of individuals form the culture
   d. Collecting oral histories
   e. Collecting documents
   f. Collecting relics
   g. Reasonable explanations, conclusions, and generalizations

32. Which of the following is *not* an extremely important measure of internal validity for qualitative research (p. 341)?
   a. History
   b. Maturation
   c. Observer/researcher effects
   d. Selection
   e. Treatment replications
   f. Attrition

33. Coding is (p. 331):
   a. the summation of the data analysis
   b. an inferential statistical technique
   c. the breaking down of large amounts of data into smaller parts
   d. Two of the above

34. Which is the correct order of the final version of a research paper (p. 349)?
   a. Abstract; review of literature; hypothesis or research questions; methodology; results, discussions, implications, and conclusions; references
   b. Review of literature; abstract; hypothesis or research questions; methodology; results, discussions, implications, and conclusions; references
   c. Hypothesis or research questions; review of literature; abstract; methodology; results, discussions, implications, and conclusions; references
   d. Abstract, hypothesis or research questions; review of literature; methodology; results, discussions, implications, and conclusions; references

35. Generally, the purpose of program evaluation is (p. 355):
   a. the examination of new paradigms to expand the understanding of knowledge
   b. the examination of past paradigms to expand the understanding of knowledge
   c. the use of inferential statistics to expand knowledge
   d. the examination of a program to see if it is worthwhile

36. Another name for formative and summative evaluation is (p. 355): (www)
   a. then and now evaluation
   b. here and there evaluation
   c. past and present evaluation
   d. process and outcome evaluation
   e. outcome and process evaluation

37. Evaluation that is concerned with assessment of a total program to see if it was worthwhile is called __________, while evaluation of a program during its implementation to see if it was worthwhile is called __________ (p. 355).
   a. summative; formative
   b. formative; summative
   c. process; outcome
   d. outcome; process
   e. Two of the above

38. Which of the following can result in cultural bias in quantitative research (p. 359)?
   a. The subject matter chosen
   b. The population chosen
   c. The design chosen
   d. The statistical analysis used
   e. Two of the above
   f. Three of the above
   g. All of the above

39. Which of the following is *not* true (p. 339)?
   a. Prior to consenting to participate in research, subjects must be told the purpose, procedures, and potential risks involved.
   b. Researchers must conduct research in a manner that respects individuals from all cultures and make reasonable efforts to assure no psychological, physical, or social injury occurs
   c. Deception in research can never be used
   d. All information obtained from research must be kept confidential

40. Which of the following is *not* a standard related to conducting research (p. 361?
   a. ACA code of ethics
   b. APA code of ethics
   c. Research curriculum standards as identified by CACREP
   d. ACES Standards on Research in Counseling

True or False

41. The literature review is an examination of current research being conducted (p. 336) **(F)**.

42. The difference between quantitative and qualitative research is minimal (p. 336) **(F)**.

43. Research designs should not be generated until the statement of the problem is formulated (p. 336) **(T)**.

44. Two main types of quantitative research are experimental and nonexperimental research (p. 337) **(T)**.

45. In historical research one hopes to show that the null hypothesis is true (p. 338) **(F)**.

46. Survey research is a type of qualitative research (p. 344) **(F)**.

47. Inferential statistics are used to describe results as measured by measures of central tendency, measures of variability, and derived scores (p. 348) **(F)**.

48. The case study method describes a method of studying a deeply probing a phenomenon or event (p. 346) **(T)**.

49. Observation in ethnographic research is usually done from the position of *participant observer* (p. 349) **(T)**.

50. Effective ethnographic interviews involve directed questioning that enables the ethnographer to get to the source of the phenomenon being studies (p. 349) **(F)**.

51. In conducting historical research, researchers never use secondary sources (p. 348) **(F)**.

52. Some suggest that rather than talking about reliability and validity in qualitative research, researchers should examine the credibility and trustworthiness of their research (p. 352) **(T)**.

53. The validity of qualitative research is partly based on the ability of the researcher to record information accurately and to use multiple methods of recording (p. 352) **(T)**.

54. Formative evaluation may employ the use of research designs while summative evaluations would not (335-356) **(F)**.

55. Because of the objective, scientific method used in quantitative research, the chances of cultural bias, as compared to qualitative research, is slim (p. 359) **(F)**.

56. Although all researchers must be concerned about cultural bias, white researchers must be much more vigilant in their effort to control bias than minority researchers (p. 360) **(T)**.

57. All organizations that receive federal funds must have an institutional review board in to assure that subjects are at little or no risk of harm when participating in research (p. 361) **(T)**.

Matching (Questions 58-69) (p. 341)

58. ___When a participant exhibits positive or negative behaviors because of the knowledge they are in a study (**J**)

59. ___When ways that subjects are selected and assigned to treatment groups effects the results (**L**)

60. ___When there is a statistical tendency for extreme scores to move closer to the mean if tested a second time (**F**)

61. ___When previously taking a test affects the results (**B**)

62. ___When external events which affects the treatment and leads to invalid conclusions (**E**)

63. ___When changes in the instrument(s) affects results (**K**)

64. ___When maturational changes such as growing older or more tired, or becoming hungry, affect the results (**H**)

65. ___When subjects have knowledge of other treatment conditions thus affecting their responses and leading to invalid results (**G**)

66. ___When the researcher treats subjects differentially based on attributes not related to the treatment (**D**)

67. ___When participants differentially drop out of treatment thus leaving only the "better" or "worse" participants (**A**)

68. ___When the number of subjects inaccurately reflects the number undergoing treatment (e.g., all subjects receive a treatment *together*) (**I**)

69. ___When a violation of statistical inferences are made (**C**)

A. Subject attrition
B. Pretesting
C. Statistical conclusions
D. Experimenter effects
E. History
F. Pretesting
G. Diffusion of treatment
H. Maturation
I. Treatment replications
J. Subject effects
K. Instrumentation
L. Selection

Matching (Questions 70-78) (pp. 337-348)

70. The independent variable is manipulated to examine its effect on the dependent variable. There is *no* random assignment to treatment groups (**I**).

71. ___When one wants or needs to avoid the use of group treatments and there is manipulation of the independent variable to see its effect on the dependent variable (**F**).

72. ___Used to gain information about the values, behaviors, demographics, and opinions of a population. Mailings and/or interviews are completed in a systematic fashion (**E**).

73. ___ Examines the relationship of already existing intact groups. Used when its impossible or impractical to manipulate the independent variable (**H**).

74. ___Used to understand events by understanding the meanings that people place on them from within their natural context (**A**).

75. ___The independent variable is manipulated to examine its effect on the dependent variable. There is random assignment to treatment groups (**B**).

76. ___Used to describe and analyze conditions and events from the past in an effort to analyze conditions and events from the past (**D**).

77. ___Used to examine the relationship between groups (**G**).

78. ___Used to determine whether or not a program has achieved its goals (**C**).

A. Ethnographic research

B. True experimental research

C. Program evaluation

D. Historical research

E. Survey research

F. Single-subject design research

G. Correlational research

H. Causal-comparative (ex-post facto research)

I. Quasi-experimental research

INFOTRAC KEY WORDS: Quantitative research. Qualitative research. Program evaluation. Ethics and counseling research.

CHAPTER 14

THEORY AND CONCEPTS OF MULTICULTURAL COUNSELING

Multiple Choice

1. Which of the following is *not* correct concerning how majority counselors tend to work with minority clients (p. 369)? (www)
   a. They tend to amplify the impact of social forces on the client
   b. They interpret cultural differences as psychopathological issues
   c. They misdiagnosis the client
   d. None of the above

2. Which is *not* true about how minority clients experience counseling (p. 369)?
   a. Because counselors have a difficult time understanding the world of the minority client, they tend to remain in therapy longer
   b. They find therapy less helpful than their majority counterparts
   c. They attend therapy at lower rates
   d. They are frequently misunderstood and often misdiagnosed

3. All of the statements listed below, except one, are reasons that counseling does *not* work for many minority clients (pp. 369-370). Pick the reason that does not make sense.
   a. Because this country is a cultural mosaic and minority clients don't have a true sense of themselves
   b. Because of incongruent expectations about counseling between counselor and client
   c. Because counselors do not understand the impact of social forces on minority clients
   d. Because counselors tend to have an ethnocentric worldview
   e. Because counselors are not always in touch with their racist attitudes and prejudices

4. All of the statements listed below, except one, are reasons that counseling does *not* work for many minority clients (pp. 369-370). Pick the reason that does not make sense.
   a. Because counselors view some cultural-specific appropriate behaviors as pathological
   b. Because assessment instruments are culturally biased and misinterpreted
   c. Because of inherent racism in society and its impact on how counselors understand the world
   d. Because counselors tend to "overcompensate" for minority clients
   e. Because counselors are not always in touch with their racist attitudes and prejudices

5. All of the following are barriers to the effective multicultural helping relationship except (pp. 369-370)?
   a. The melting pot myth
   b. Understanding the universality of symptomatology
   c. Having incongruent expectations about counseling
   d. Lacking an understanding of social forces
   e. Having an ethnocentric worldview
   f. Being ignorant of self-racism and other's cultural identity

6. Which of the following best represents the concept of having an ethnocentric worldview (p. 370)?
   a. It means that we have examined our prejudices, and stereotypes, understand our beliefs, have a knowledge base, and have the skills necessary to work with clients of diverse backgrounds.
   b. It means that the helper assumes that their way of viewing the world is the same as the client's.
   c. It means that we have participated in Pedersen's (1981, 1983) triad model.
   d. It means that we are developmentally mature as it pertains to counseling clients of diverse backgrounds.

7. Which of the following values is *not* stressed by traditional views of counseling (p. 369)? (www)
   a. Cause and effect
   b. Mind/body integration
   c. Self-disclosure
   d. Open-mindedness and insight
   e. Focus on the individual

8. Which of the following represents the classical definition of race (p. 372)?
   a. A grouping of people based on similar genetics and biology
   b. The common values, norms of behavior, symbols, language, and life patterns that people may share
   c. The sharing of a common ancestry which includes specific cultural and social patterns, not necessarily based on genetic heritage
   d. All of the above

9. Which of the following represents the classical definition of culture (p. 371)?
   a. A grouping of people based on similar genetics and biology
   b. The common values, norms of behavior, symbols, language, and life patterns that people may share
   c. The sharing of a common ancestry which includes specific cultural and social patterns, not necessarily based on genetic heritage
   d. All of the above

10. Which of the following represents the classical definition of ethnicity (p. 372)?
   a. A grouping of people based on similar genetics and biology
   b. The common values, norms of behavior, symbols, language, and life patterns that people may share
   c. The sharing of a common ancestry which includes specific cultural and social patterns, not necessarily based on genetic heritage
   d. All of the above

11. Tom is Asian-American and a supervisor in a large engineering firm. His employees, have a history of not getting along with their supervisors in the past, regardless of their ethnic background. They do not like Tom. Most likely this is an example of (p. 373):
   a. discrimination b. social class differences c. power differentials d. racism.

12. Even though Julie is pleasant when around men, with her friends she says that "all men are nasty, self-centered, and out for only one thing--sex." She is exhibiting which of the following (p. 373)?
   a. Racism
   b. Power differentials
   c. Discrimination
   c. Social class differences
   d. Stereotyping

13. Jonathan is Jewish, so you assume that he only eats Kosher food. You are (p. 373):
   a. Being ethnocentric
   b. Being racist
   c. Discriminating against a person
   d. Having incongruent expectations about the helping relationship
   e. Jumping to conclusions and stereotyping

14. The most recent hate crime statistics reveals all but which of the following (p. 374)? (www)
   a. The largest percentage of hate crimes are motivated by racial bias
   b. About 11% of hate crimes were based on one's ethnicity/national origin
   c. Over 15% of hate crimes were for sexual orientation
   d. A surprisingly large percentage of hate crimes were against whites

15. Which of the following terms is correctly matched (p. 375)?
   a. Eigenwelt–Cultural Commonality
   b. Mitwelt–Human Universality
   c. Umwelt–Individual uniqueness
   d. None of the above are correctly matched
   e. All of the above are correctly matched

16. Which is most likely to hinder our work with clients of diverse backgrounds (p. 369)?
   a. If we endorse white identity models of development
   b. If we place some emphasis on how social and environmental factors affect our clients
   c. If we have examined our own prejudices and racist attitudes
   d. If we view American society as a melting pot

17. Angela is Hispanic by birth but has no awareness of her cultural background. In fact, when people ask her about her heritage, she says "I'm American." According to Bell (1981), Angela has a way of relating to the world called an(n) (p. 376):
   a. acculturated interpersonal style
   b. bi-cultural interpersonal style
   c. culturally immersed interpersonal style
   d. traditional interpersonal style

18. Minority identity models do all but which of the following (p. 376-377)?
   a. They help counselors understand his or her biases
   b. They help counselors better understand the minority client
   c. They assist minority counselors in understanding minority clients
   d. They assist minority counselors in understanding themselves
   e. All of the above

19. In Bell's minority identity model, the individual who is guarded, often a radical or political activist, usually intelligent and often blaming of society has a way of relating to the world called a(n) (p. 376):
   a. acculturated interpersonal style
   b. bi-cultural interpersonal style
   c. culturally immersed interpersonal style
   d. traditional interpersonal style

20. Thomas is African American but can easily relate to whites and blacks. According to Bell, this is a person has a way of relating to the world called a(n) (p. 376): (www)
   a. acculturated interpersonal style
   b. bi-cultural interpersonal style
   c. culturally immersed interpersonal style
   d. traditional interpersonal style

21. Atkinson, Morten, and Sue's minority identity model can help counselors understand all but which of the following (p. 377)?
   a. The nature of identity development for minorities
   b. The role oppression plays with minorities
   c. The reasons for prejudice, discrimination, and racism
   d. Differences *within* a culture
   e. The potential for change in a minority client

22. The correct order of stages of Atkinson, Morten, and Sue's (1998) minority identity model is (p. 377):
   a. conformity, dissonance, resistance and immersion, introspection, synergetic articulation
   b. dissonance, conformity, resistance and immersion, introspection, synergetic articulation
   c. resistance and immersion, dissonance, conformity, introspection, synergetic articulation
   d. resistance and immersion, conformity, dissonance, introspection, synergetic articulation

23. Dale, who is white, is an ardent supporter of minority concerns. He often can be found actively involved in protests and legislative actions. He also has a tendency to put down his "whiteness." He is in which of Sabnani, Ponterotto's, and Borodovsky's (1991) white identity model (p. 377-378)?
   a. Stage 1, pre-exposure
   b. Stage 2, exposure
   c. Stage 3, prominority/antiracism
   d. Stage 4, retreat to white culture
   e. Stage 5, redefinition and integration

24. Mary Ann is hostile and fearful of minorities. She had been very supportive, but rejection from some minority groups has led her to want to disengage from prominority stances. She is in which of Sabnani, Ponterotto's, and Borodovsky's white identity model (pp. 377-378)?
   a. Stage 1, pre-exposure
   b. Stage 2, exposure
   c. Stage 3, prominority/antiracism
   d. Stage 4, retreat to white culture
   e. Stage 5, redefinition and integration

25. The redefinition and integration stage of Sabnani, Ponterotto's, and Borodovsky's white identity model is highlighted by (pp. 377-378) which of the following:
   a. hostility toward minority groups
   b. early exposure and beginning awareness of other cultural groups
   c. hostility followed by acceptance of minority groups
   d. a world view of multiculturalism

26. When assisting a culturally different client, it is important to (p. 380-382):
   a. understand that counseling is not fixed, but a constantly changing process
   b. that the helping relationship is an active process that is ongoing
   c. recognize the complexity and diversity of the client and client populations and acknowledge our own personal limitations and the need to always improve
   d. All of the above

27. To effectively work with a culturally diverse population, skilled mental-health workers must (pp. 380-382):
   a. be aware of their attitudes and beliefs toward culturally diverse populations
   b. have a knowledge base that supports their work with diverse clients
   c. have the necessary skills to apply to clients with diverse backgrounds
   d. All of the above

28. Relative to the future of multicultural counseling, Essandoh (1996) suggests that (p. 382):
   a. Multicultural counseling may be a "fourth force"
   b. The process of applying theory to practice in multicultural counseling has been slow
   c. Professionals and professional associations need to actively pursue the advancement of multicultural issues
   d. Two of the Above
   e. All of the above

29. The *Multicultural Counseling Competencies and Standards* represent which of the following (p. 383)?
   a. Ethical guidelines when doing multicultural counseling
   b. Guidelines for understanding one's cultural identity
   c. Accreditation guidelines for multicultural counseling
   d. Minimum standards needed by counselors if they are to work effectively with diverse clients

30. Which of the following is (was) one of the leaders in the field of multicultural counseling (p. 382)?
   a. Virginia Satir   b. Ashram Magir   c. Malcolm X   **d.** Derald Sue

31. Which association has developed competencies for multicultural counseling (384)?
   a. AMCD   b. AHEAD   c. ACA   d. ASERVIC   e. ACES

32. What is the function of the anticounselor in Pederson's (1981, 1983) triad model (p. 384)?
   a. To assist the client in his or her understanding of the counselor's culture
   b. To explain to the counselor the techniques that he or she is using that may be biased
   c. To provide one-to-one supervision to the counselor
   d. To highlight the differences in values and expectations between the client and counselor

33. Which of the following should counselors *not* do if they are to act ethically (p. 385)? (www)
   a. Assist clients in advocating for their rights
   b. Advocate for the client
   c. Campaign for legislative initiatives
   d. Understand legal issues
   e. Two of the above
   f. None of the above (the counselor should do all of the above)

True or False

34. A counselor must possess specific knowledge about the client's cultural or ethnic group but at the same time not assume that just because a client comes from a specific cultural background that he or she necessarily has these characteristics (pp. 369-370) (**T**).

35. Issues of racism, discrimination, and other social forces "outside" of the individual have little effect on the client's ability to make changes in his or her life because change is within the individual (p. 369) (**F**).

(*) One of the biggest reasons helping professionals struggle with diversity issues is the: (a) interpretation of situations from personal worldview

36. Race represents the common values, life patterns, language, symbols, and norms of behavior that a group may share (p. 322) (**F**).

37. Ethnicity is based on genetic heritage (p. 372) (**F**).

38. Social class has been called the "missing dimension" in understanding diversity and has been largely overlooked (p. 373) (**T**).

39. In some societies, power differentials may create greater disparities among people than culture, ethnic group, race, or social class (p. 373) (**T**).

40. Women are a minority (p. 373) (**T**).

41. A minority is any group which is being singled out due to their cultural or physical characteristics, are being systematically oppressed, and who represent less than 50% of the population (p. 373) (**F**).

42. Counselors should practice political correctness when it comes to referring to ethnic and cultural groups (p. 375) (**T**).

43. The culturally sensitive counselor takes into account the universal experiences, cultural specificity, and individual uniqueness of the client (p. 375) (**T**).

44. The minority identity model of Atkinson, Morten, and Sue ranges from emersion in the dominant culture, through emersion in the minority culture, to pride and acceptance of one's own cultural identity as well as the ability to accept or reject values from other cultures (p. 377) (**T**).

45. Whereas Bell's minority identity model is developmental, the model of Atkinson, Morten, and Sue is stagnant (pp. 375-377) (**F**).

46. Early research seems to indicate that development of white identity may be positively correlated with the ability to work with diverse clients (p. 377) (**T**).

47. D'Andrea's highest stage of white identity development suggests that individuals must actively work toward system change (p. 379) (**T**).

48. In order to effectively work with a culturally different client it is essential that you hold the same belief system as he or she does (pp. 380-382) (**F**).

49. Working with culturally different clients should be viewed as understanding a distinct body of knowledge and skills that will change little over time (pp. 380-382) (**F**).

50. Standards focused on multicultural counseling training seem necessary for counselor education programs because of the complexity of multicultural counselor training (pp. 383-384) (**T**).

51. Although training models exist to help counselors work with minority clients, it is still unclear as to whether they are enough to make a significant difference (p. 384) (**T**).

INFOTRAC KEY WORDS: Minority identity models. Efficacy of counseling minorities. Race. Culture. Prejudice.

b) realization that everyone is the same
c) understanding that asking questions is healthy
d) none of the above

CHAPTER 15

KNOWLEDGE AND SKILLS OF MULTICULTURAL COUNSELING

Multiple Choice

1. Currently, ______ percent of Americans are racial and ethnic minorities, and midway into the 21st century______ percent of the country will be minorities (p. 389).
   a. 15; 25   b. 25; 30   c. 30; 50   d. 30; 75   e. 50; 75

2. The minority group that will see the largest percent increase in the 21st century will be (p. 389): (www)
   a. African Americans
   b. Hispanics
   c. American Indian
   d. Asians

3. Which of the following is not a reason for the changing demographics as we move into the 21st century (p. 389)?
   a. Changing immigration patterns
   b. Higher birth rates of culturally diverse populations
   c. Higher immigration rates than in the past
   d. Two of the above
   e. All of the above

4. How many Africans may have died from the deplorable conditions on the slave ships (p. 390)? (www)
   a. 1 million
   b. 1-3 million
   c. 3-5 million
   d. 5-8 million
   e. 6-10 million

5. What percentage of African Americans are descendant from slaves (p. 390)?
   a. 25%   b. 35%   c. 60%   d. 90%

6. This act, passed in 1991, protected minority workers from discriminatory practices in employment (p. 391).
   a. Americans with Disabilities Act
   b. Carl Perkins Act
   c. The Buckley Amendment
   d. Civil Rights Act

7. What percentage of hate crimes reported are committed against African Americans (p. 391)?
   a. 15%   b. 22%   c. 38%   d. 58%   e. 78%

8. Which of the following tends *not* to be true of African Americans (p. 391)?
   a. They are group oriented and value cooperation and interdependence
   b. The extended family is varied and important
   c. Family matters are kept within the family or extended family
   d. Mental health problems tend to be somaticized

9. Some reasons that many Hispanics have a difficult time acculturating and becoming upwardly mobile include all but which of the following (p. 392)?
   a. A shared common language with other Hispanics makes it easier to maintain a separate culture
   b. Many Hispanics have not established roots due to the proximity of their countries of origin
   c. In general, Hispanics do not value education
   d. As compared to past immigrants, today there is a lack of opportunity for immigrants

10. All but which of the following are some values and customs shared by many Hispanics (p. 392)?
    a. Hispanic families tend to be matriarchal
    b. Individuals are respected based on age, status, gender, and socioeconomic status
    c. Many Hispanics deeply embrace traditional Catholic values
    d. Many Hispanics believe in cultural fatalism, or the belief that life is out of one's control

11. Which of the following are not countries from Asia or the Pacific Islands (p. 393)?
   a. Philippines
   b. Korea
   c. Hawaii
   d. India
   e. China
   f. Japan
   g. Two of the above
   h. None of the above (all are from Asia or the Pacific Islands)

12. Which is not true? During the second World War, many Japanese (p. 393):
   a. were interned in camps
   b. moved to the Midwest if they promised not to live on the west coast.
   c. found to be spies for Japan
   d. Two of the above are not true
   e. All of the above are not true

13. Which of the following is not true (p. 393)?
   a. Many Chinese came to the United States during the gold rush
   b. The United States set up colonial rule in the Philippines following the end of the Spanish-American War
   c. Surprisingly, few Koreans and Vietnamese emigrated to this country following the end of the Korean and Vietnam wars
   d. Many Asians settled in the United States during the late 1800s

14. All but which of the following are some values and customs shared by many Asians and Pacific Islanders (p. 393)?
   a. Children tend to be obligated to parents and place them first
   b. Families tend to be patriarchal
   c. Family members tend to be highly interdependent
   d. Guilt and shame are often used to control the behavior of family members
   e. Restrain and the ability to control feelings is highly valued
   f. Informality in social relationships is the norm

15. Native Americans include all but which of the following (p. 394):
   a. American Indians
   b. Aleuts
   c. Eskimos
   d. Mayans

16. Which of the following was not responsible for the death of millions of American Indians during the colonization of America (p. 394)?
   a. Diseases brought over from Europe
   b. Wars
   c. Alcoholism
   d. All of the above were responsible

17. American Indians tend to (p. 394):
   a. view mental health problems from a spiritual and holistic perspective
   b. see problems as an extension of the community
   c. use ceremony, storytelling, and metaphor in understanding the individual
   d. have unique traditions based on their tribal affiliation
   e. All of the above

18. In working with individuals from different cultures, which should not be done (p. 395)?
   a. Encourage clients to speak their own language
   b. Know the cultural heritage of your client
   c. Assess the cultural identity of your client using a minority identity model
   d. Make assumptions about the client based on his or her nonverbal behavior
   e. Use alternative forms of communication

19. Which of the following *may* be inappropriate when working with clients from a different culture (p. 395)?
   a. To meet with clients outside of your office to aid in comfort level
   b. To encourage clients to bring items from home in order to help you understand their culture
   c. To make sure you are looking directly at your clients so they know you are attending to them
   d. None of the above

20. Which of the following statements is true (p. 395)?
   a. The religious makeup of the United States has remained fairly stable over the past two decades
   b. There are between 10 and 20 religious groups in the United States that have more than 50,000 members
   c. Ninety-eight percent (98%) of Americans claim a religious affiliation
   d. Eighty-five percent (85%) of Americans state that religion is fairly or very important to them.

21. Relative to Christianity, which of the following statements is true (p. 396)?
   a. Differences among Christian churches are minimal around the world
   b. The teaching of Jesus was consolidated into the Old and New Testaments
   c. Over the centuries, interpretation of the Gospel has varied greatly as a function of the religious leader or scholar.
   d. There are approximately a dozen Christian sects all of which espouse slightly different forms of Christianity

22. Which of the following nonauthoritarian religions professes five duties: to pray five times a day, to give regularly to charity, to fast daily during one month a year, and to make one pilgrimage to their holy place during their lifetime (p. 397)?
   a. Christianity b. Buddhism c. Judaism d. Hinduism e. Islam

23. Which of the following religions believes that reality is an illusion (p. 396)?
   a. Christianity b. Buddhism c. Judaism d. Hinduism e. Islam

24. Which of the following religions believes that there is one divine principle--that many gods are aspects of a single divine unity and that one can be improved through pure actions and meditation and become close to the divine (p. 397)? (www)
   a. Christianity b. Buddhism c. Judaism d. Hinduism e. Islam

25. Which religions that coalesced around the year 1300 B.C. E. sees its purpose as transforming what is into what should be, believes in peace and cooperation, love and acceptance of others, and a progressive view toward life (p. 397)?
   a. Christianity b. Buddhism c. Judaism d. Hinduism e. Islam

26. In working with clients, which of the following is important in reference to the client's religion (p. 398)?
   a. It is important to wait before determining a client's religious background so one does not offend the client.
   b. One should avoid asking the client how religion is important in his or her life
   c. It is important to assess the client's faith development (e.g., Fowler)
   d. Two of the above
   e. Three of the above

27. Which is *not* true (p. 399)?
   a. Women have higher death rates than men.
   b. Men are doing less child care today than 20 years ago.
   c. Women are less likely to finish college than men.
   d. Elderly women are less likely to commit suicide than elderly men.
   e. a and b
   f. c and d

28. Which association has developed principles for counselors when working with women (p. 400)?
   a. ACA b. APA d. NASW e. NOHSE

29. As compared to some feminist counselors, a more radical approach to working with women includes which of the following (p. 400)?
   a. Suggest that the repressed female client get in touch with her anger and act it out by joining organizations like NOW and through acts of civil disobedience
   b. Advise female clients that the world is male-dominated and hostile toward women and suggest that they begin to act in a manner that will acknowledge this fact
   c. Suggest that women deal with conflicting feelings they may have between traditional and newfound values discovered in counseling
   d. Two of the above

30. Which is *not* true about the women's movement (p. 402)? (www)
   a. It has advanced women's issues
   b. It has helped sensitize men
   c. It has resulted in some therapists having negative attitudes toward mens' issues
   d. None of the above (all of the above are true)

31. In regards to counseling men, at varying times in the counseling relationship the counselor will act in all but which of the following ways (p. 403)?
   a. Accept men where they are and don't push them to express "softer feelings"
   b. Validate the man's view of how he has been constrained by male sex-role stereotypes
   c. Be nondirective throughout the counseling relationship
   d. Discuss developmental issues
   e. Encourage the expression of new feelings
   f. Reinforce new ways of understanding the world

32. Gender aware therapy suggests all but which of the following (p. 404)?
   a. Reinforce traditional gender roles
   b. View problems within a societal context
   c. Develop a collaborative and equal relationship
   d. Actively address gender injustices

33. Which of the following did the Kinsey studies not show (p. 404)?
   a. That 50% of males have had some sexual history with other males
   b. That you either are, or are not gay or straight, there is nothing in between
   c. That 8% of men are exclusively homosexual for three years of their lives between the ages of 16 and 55
   d. That 4% of men are exclusively homosexual throughout their lives

34. Which is *not* true about homophobics (p. 404)?
   a. They are most likely hiding from their own homosexuality
   b. They might be distorting reality because of fears concerning their own sexuality
   c. Some homophobics may act out toward gays and lesbians
   d. They are most likely holding prejudicial attitudes

35. Which of the following is true about transvestism (p. 405)?
   a. It is synonymous with transsexualism
   b. It tends to be found almost exclusively in the homosexual population
   c. It is not too common among gay men
   d. It is an illness
   e. Two of the above

36. When counseling gay men and lesbian women, which of the following is *not* true (p. 406)? (www)
   a. Make assumptions about the lifestyle, this will help the gay or lesbian client to open up about his or her sexuality
   b. Be tuned into domestic violence issues, as they can occur in gay and lesbian relationships as they do in heterosexual ones
   c. Be aware that gay men and lesbian clients may have a greater tendency toward abusing substances
   d. Be aware that compared to heterosexual women, a larger percent of lesbian women have probably been sexually abused

37. In reference to AIDS, which of the following is *not* true (pp. 406-407)?
   a. The U.S. Supreme Court has stated that insurance companies must provide payments for individuals with chronic illnesses
   b. The number of individuals contracting the HIV virus is increasing
   c. Counselors will most likely find themselves increasingly working with individuals who have contracted the AIDS virus
   d. Prevention and education are particularly important when dealing with the spread of the AIDS virus

38. In what areas of the HIV positive and AIDS epidemic might you find a counselor working (pp. 407-408)?
   a. Prevention and education programs
   b. Counseling of survivors of AIDS, family members, and friends
   c. Counseling HIV positive and AIDS infected individuals
   d. Supervisors of volunteers and paraprofessionals who work with HIV individuals
   e. All of the above

39. Which is *not* important when working with individuals who are HIV positive (pp. 407-408)?
   a. Knowing the cultural background of the individual
   b. Knowing about the disease, and myths that go along with it
   c. Being in roles that are not typical of counselors (e.g., advocating, caretaking)
   d. Dealing with issues of loss for the client *and* for the counselor
   e. None of the above (all are important)

40. What did the McKinney Act provide (p. 408)?
   a. Job training and counseling for the poor
   b. Child care programs for the poor
   c. Vocational services for individuals with a disability
   d. Transportation services for individuals with a disability
   e. a and b
   f. c and d

41. Which of the following is usually of less a concern when counseling the homeless and the poor (pp. 408-409)?
   a. Social issues
   b. Cultural issues
   c. Health risks
   d. Multiple problems
   e. Developmental delays
   f. Psychological problems
   g. Limited resources for referrals

42. In 2000, about __________ percent of the country were over 65, and in 2035 about __________ percent of the country will be over 65 (pp. 409-410). (www)
   a. 5; 10 b. 10; 14 c. 13; 20 d. 20;35 e. 30; 35

43. Which of the following should the counselor *not* be concerned about when counseling older persons (p. 410)? (www)
   a. Mistrust of counselors by the elderly
   b. Depression
   c. Identity issues
   d. Health issues
   e. Interpersonal relationships
   f. Sexual dysfunction
   g. None of the above (all should be of concern)

44. Which of the following has *not* decreased the number of individuals being admitted to state mental hospitals (p. 411)?
   a. The Community Mental Health Centers Act of 1963
   b. The use of psychotropic medications
   c. The U.S. Supreme Court decision in Donaldson v. O'Connor
   d. The decrease in the number of mentally ill in the country

45. All but which of the following should be considered when counseling the mentally ill (pp..411-412)?
   a. Helping the client understand and work through his or her feelings about the illness
   b. Attendance in counseling
   c. Compliance with medication
   d. Assuring accurate diagnosis
   e. Reevaluating treatment plans
   f. Family involvement
   g. Knowing resources
   h. None of the above (all should be considered)

46. Which of the following did the Americans with Disabilities Act of 1992 *not* do (p. 413)?.
   a. Assured the right of individuals with disabilities to receive vocational rehabilitation
   b. Ensured that qualified individuals with disabilities cannot be discriminated against on the job
   c. Required the modifying of equipment, on the job, for individuals with disabilities
   d. Ensured that existing facilities used by employees be accessible for individuals with disabilities

47. Which of the following should *not* be of done when counseling individuals with disabilities (p. 413)?
   a. Knowledge of disabilities
   b. Assisting clients in learning about their disability
   c. Assisting clients through the grieving process
   d. Knowing laws and resources
   e. Potentially doing vocational/career counseling about their loss
   f. Including the family
   g. Advocating for the client
   h. Confronting the client directly in an effort to have him or her deal with the disability

48. In reference to learning about different cultural groups, which of the following is correct (p. 414)?
   a. It may lead to stereotyping and generalizing a people from a culture and ultimately, failures in counseling
   b. It could lead to a self-fulfilling prophecy, whereby clients act in a certain manner because we believe they should act that way
   c. Increased sensitivity of clients and more effective counseling
   d. Counselors may adapt new styles of relating to clients which are more effective
   e. Two of the above
   f. All of the above

True and False

49. About thirteen percent of Americans (37 million) are African American (p. 390) (**T**).

50. The great majority of immigrants today are African and Hispanic (p. 389) (**F**).

51. In the early 1970s, laws restricting access for minorities to education, work, and recreational facilities still existed in many states (p. 391) (**T**).

52. Whereas some African Americans may be defensive and guarded with whites, these same individuals may be expressive, open, and responsive with other African Americans (pp. 391-392) (**T**).

53. Many Mexican Americans came to this country as slaves during the 1700s (p. 392) (**F**)

54. Kwanzaa is a celebration of freedom and liberty (p. 391) (**F**).

55. African Americans vary widely in their connectedness to their culture, and one must assess the degree to which their culture affects them if one is to work effectively with a black client (p. 391) (**T**).

56. Although Puerto Rico is a Commonwealth of the United States, Puerto Ricans do not have citizenship (p. 392) (**F**).

57. The majority of Cubans came to the United States during the Spanish American war at in 1898 (p. 392) (**F**).

58. Few Hispanics in the United States come from Central or South America (p. 392) (**F**).

59. In working with Hispanics, the similarities in cultures are so great that knowledge of specific cultures need not be known (p. 392) (**F**).

60. Chinatowns today are a sign of the upward economic mobility of the Chinese in this country (p. 393) (**F**).

61. In working with individuals from Asia and the Pacific Islands, the similarities in culture are so great that knowledge of specific cultures need not be known (p. 394) (**F**).

62. Approximately one-half of American Indians live on reservations (p. 394) (**T**).

63. Today, there are more than 150 American Indian tribal languages and 900 federal and state-recognized tribes (p. 374) (**T**).

64. American Indians tend to overutilize mental health services (p. 394) (**F**).

65. There is little or no relationship between religious affiliation and social class, culture, ethnicity, race, and political attitudes (p. 355) (**F**).

66. In many minority cultures the extended family plays a crucial role (pp. 390-394) (**T**).

67. Because we live in an increasingly tolerant country, concerns over acceptance of gays and lesbians by religious groups has been minimal (p. 406) (**F**).

68. Approximately two billion people in the world identifies themselves as Christian (p. 396) (**T**).

69. Approximately 18% of the world identifies themselves as Muslim (p. 396) (**T**).

70. Approximately 13% of the world identifies themselves as Hindu (p. 396) (**T**).

71. Approximately 6% of the world identifies themselves as Buddhists (p. 396) (**T**).

72. Many clients are influenced by their religious upbringing in unconscious ways (p. 398) (**T**).

73. Recent research indicates that there are probably few personality differences between men and women (p. 399) (**F**).

74. Early in the counseling relationship with men, it is probably smart to gently push them into expressing "softer" feelings (p. 402) (**F**).

75. Even though the American Psychological Association views homosexuality as an alternative lifestyle, 62% of Americans believe homosexuals should not have the right to marry (p. 405) (**T**).

76. Sexual orientation is probably learned, not biologically determined (p. 404) (**F**).

77. Close to five million Americans have the AIDS virus (p. 406) (**F**).

78. Although not the perception of many, the rate of homelessness and poverty is the same for all ethnic and cultural groups (p. 408) (**F**).

79. Due to the isolation of the homeless and poor from the rest of society, it is not surprising that they are at a greater risk of developing AIDS, tuberculosis, and other diseases (p. 409) (**T**).

80. An indication of the increased mental health of the American population is the decrease in numbers of inpatients in psychiatric hospitals (p. 411) (**F**).

81. Some people say that as many as 20% to 60% of the homeless may have severe psychiatric problems (p. 411) (**T**).

82. The Rehabilitation Act of 1973 ensures access to vocational rehabilitation services for the severely mentally or physically disabled (p. 413) (T).

83. It is estimated that 1 in 6 Americans are born with a disability (p. 412) (T).

84. Some have suggested that the revised ACA ethical guidelines continue to be biased toward the dominant culture (p. 415) (T).

85. The use of ethical guidelines or moral decision making models may be biased when doing cross-cultural counseling (p. 415) (T).

Fill in the Blank (Questions 86-99)
List seven concerns of women and seven concerns of men which should be considered when counseling them (pp. 399, 404):

Concerns of Women		Concerns of Men	
86.	______________	93.	______________
87.	______________	94.	______________
88.	______________	95.	______________
89.	______________	96.	______________
90.	______________	97.	______________
91.	______________	98.	______________
92.	______________	99.	______________

INFOTRAC KEY WORDS: Effective multicultural counseling. Counseling minorities. Counseling women. Counseling gays. Counseling lesbians.

CHAPTER 16

SCHOOL COUNSELING

1. The first school counselors were (p. 421):
   a. developed out of a need for moral guidance
   b. a response to the increased need for vocational guidance
   c. the result of Sputnik
   d. None of the above

2. Parsons approach to counseling was based on all but which of the following (p. 421):
   a. understanding developmental stages
   b. understanding self
   c. knowledge of the principles of success
   d. knowledge of the occupational information
   e. the ability to make a reasoned choice between one's understanding of self and one's understanding of the world of work

3. Which of the following was not important to the establishment of school counseling as a profession (p. 422)?
   a. The vocational guidance movement
   b. The Wagner O'Day Act
   c. The establishment of the U. S. Employment Service
   d. The spread of the use of assessment instruments
   e. None of the above (they all were responsible for the establishment of counseling)

4. Who suggested that guidance counselors be involved in more than vocational guidance (p. 422)?
   a. Frank Parsons
   b. John Brewer
   c. E. G. Williamson
   d. Carl Rogers

5. The Minnesota Point of View developed by E. G. Williamson was (p. 422): (www)
   a. one of the first comprehensive approaches to counseling
   b. directive
   c. shaped the practice of school counseling
   d. Two of the above
   e. All of the above

6. During the 1940s school counseling was shaped by which of the following (p. 422):
   a. the directive approach of E. G. Williamson
   b. the psychoanalytic approach of the neo-Freudians
   c. the educational reform movement
   d. the humanistic approach of Carl Rogers

7. Which of the following was not an important event that shaped the direction of school counseling during the 1950s (pp. 421-424)?
   a. The formation of ASCA
   b. The formation of NCDA and ACES
   c. The launching of Sputnik and the subsequent passage of the NDEA
   d. The passage of the Elementary and Secondary Education Act

8. Today, the major focus of school counseling includes all but which of the following (p. 424)? (www)
   a. Consultation
   b. Counseling
   c. Coordination
   d. Guidance
   e. Teaching

9. A preplanned activity based on identified developmental needs of students describes which of the following (p. 424)?
   a. Group Guidance
   b. Coordination
   c. Group Counseling
   d. Consultation
   e. Teaching

10. A one-to-one personal interaction between the student and the counselor, focusing on a particular topic describes which of the following (p. 425)?
   a. Individual Guidance
   b. Coordination
   c. Individual Counseling
   d. Consultation
   e. Teaching

11. An interaction between the counselor and four to eight students to explore a common issue describes which of the following (p. 426)?
   a. Group Guidance
   b. Coordination
   c. Group Counseling
   d. Consultation
   e. Teaching

12. The process that involves the counselor working with a teacher, parent, or other professional who shares concerns about a child to explore new ways of working with that child is called (p. 426):
   a. Guidance
   b. Coordination
   c. Counseling
   d. Consultation
   e. Teaching

13. When the counselor assumes a leadership role in managing indirect services that could benefit students it is called (p. 426):
   a. guidance
   b. coordination
   c. counseling
   d. consultation
   e. teaching

14. Which of the following theoretical approaches is most likely to be taken on by a school counselor (p. 427)?
   a. Psychodynamic
   b. Person-centered
   c. Gestalt
   d. REBT
   e. Brief-treatment

15. What approach to school counseling is generally suggested today (p. 427)? (www)
   a. Directive and focused
   b. Client-centered, deterministic
   c. Comprehensive developmental
   d. Person-centered facilitative
   e. Programmatic guidance

16. Which of the following is not suggested by a comprehensive developmental guidance and counseling program (p. 427)?
   a. A major focus on mental health services offered by the school counselor
   b. Support learning and involve teachers
   c. Proactive involvement
   d. Developmental, preventive, and remedial
   e. Individual and group counseling and guidance, coordination and consultation
   f. The belief that each child can reach his or her potential

17. Neukrug, Bar, Hoffman, & Kaplan's (1993) comprehensive developmental counseling and guidance model suggests which of the following steps (p. 428)?
   a. Planning the program, designing the program, implementing the program
   b. Assessing, designing, implementing, evaluating
   c. Designing, implementing, evaluating
   d. All of the above

18. The student to counselor ratio in many states approaches which of the following (p. 429)?
   a. 1: 50
   b. 1: 100
   c. 1: 250
   d. 1: 500

19. In comparing elementary, middle, and secondary school counseling, which of the following is true (p. 429)? (www)
   a. Secondary school counselors are much more involved in testing than elementary or middle school counselors
   b. Elementary school counselors do much more individual counseling than high school counselors
   c. Secondary school counselors do much more administrative and clerical work than either elementary or middle school counselors
   d. Elementary school counselors do significant more guidance activities than middle or secondary school counselors
   e. a and b
   f. c and d
   g. All of the above

20. One of the most effective means of working with children in elementary schools which is used more frequently than in middle or high schools is (p. 431):
   a. individual counseling
   b. assessment interpretation
   c. small group counseling
   d. consultation
   e. coordination

21. The argument for middle schools over junior high schools had to do with which of the following (p. 432)?
   a. The fact that children were growing up more quickly
   b. The fact that it made more sense from a developmental task perspective
   c. The fact that it made more sense from an economic perspective in that you could have more equal numbers of students in elementary and middle schools
   d. Two of the above
   e. All of the above

22. Which of the following developmental tasks are middle school counselors *not* concerned with (p. 433)?
   a. General increase in autonomy
   b. Sense of identity through comparison of self with others
   c. Increased concern about peer relationships
   d. Dramatic physical and emotional changes
   e. Making career choices

23. Which of the following roles is *not* carried out by the middle school counselor (p. 433)?
   a. Individual and group counseling
   b. Identifying and referring students with special needs
   c. Helping students make good educational choices and providing support for students with academic problems
   d. Providing career guidance activities
   e. Working with administrators to assist in placement of students
   f. Interpreting data for teachers, parents, and administrators
   g. None of the above (all is carried out by the middle school counselor)

24. Which of the following roles is *not* carried out by the secondary school counselor (p. 435)?
   a. Provide individual and group counseling
   b. Provide assistance with scheduling of classes for students
   c. Assist in planning for work roles and for college
   d. Provide prevention programs
   e. Consult with teachers, administrators, other professionals, and parents regarding student concerns and developmental issues
   f. Perform needs assessments and evaluate programs
   g. Sit on special education teams
   h. None of the above (the secondary school counselor performs all of these roles)

25. The DeWitt Wallace-Reader's Digest grant suggests a new vision of school counseling that changes school counselors from having a focus on ___________ to have a focus on ____________ (p. 437).
   a. mental health problems; academic and student achievement
   b. student deficit; student strengths
   c. ancillary support professional; integral member of educational team
   d. group data to effect change; one-on-one focus to effect change
   e. service providers; advocates and leaders

26. Which is not stressed by the National Standards for School Counseling Programs (p. 437)? (www)
   a. academic development
   b. career development
   c. intrapsychic development
   d. personal/social development

27. As we move into the next millennium, which is not a new role school counselors are likely to find themselves in (pp. 437-439)?
   a. Counselor as information manager
   b. Advocate for ALL students
   c. Educational leader
   d. Multicultural expert
   e. Two of the above
   f. Three of the above
   g. All of the above are new roles

28. The counselor of the 21st century will increasingly be faced with creating a multicultural school environment. Which of the following would you expect such a counselor to *not* be doing (pp. 439-440)?
   a. Counselors may need to use interpreters or find third-party assistance when working with non English-speaking students
   b. Advocate for minorities and the poor
   c. Offer workshops and programs to sensitize school personnel and develop a multiculturally attuned environment which feels safe for ALL students
   d. Evaluate guidance materials to assure cross-cultural appropriateness
   e. Assist parents of minority students to feel included in the educational experience of their child
   f. None of the above (the school counselor will be doing all of the above)

29. Relative to ethical and professional issues, which is true (pp. 440-441)?
   a. ASCA has decided to rescind its ethical guidelines in favor of ACAs code.
   b. ASCA has developed "Tips for Counselors" which highlight some major ethical and professional issues
   c. ASCA has developed a network of counseling resources
   d. a and b
   e. b and c
   f. All of the above

30. A six-year-old child is given a test, at the school's expense, to determine if the child has a learning disability in math. The child is then referred to a math specialist for tutoring, for one-hour a week, three times a week. This scenario reflects which of the following laws (p. 442)?
   a. The American for Disabilities Act
   b. The Buckley Amendment
   c. The Freedom of Information Act
   d. Public Law 94-142 (PL94-142)

True or False

31. The Wagner O'Day Act was responsible for the establishment of the U. S. Employment Service (p. 422) (**T**).

32. The 1940s saw school counseling broaden its perspective to include mental health counseling, consultation and coordination (p. 422) (**T**).

33. The Elementary and Secondary Education Act and Vocational Education Act focused on the development of services for the gifted so that school counselors could identify young people who had math and science talent (p. 423) (**F**).

34. One major change that occurred during the 1960s, 1970s, and 1980s was the focus of school counseling on developmental issues (p. 423) (**T**).

35. Counseling in the schools is almost always short-term (p. 427) (**T**).

36. Generally, parents do not have the right to counseling information about their child. This is confidential. (p. 442) (**F**).

37. An integrative approach to elementary school counseling means that counselors attempt to address an array of issues when working with the developmental needs of children (p. 427) (**T**).

38. The DeWitt Wallace-Readers Digest grant *Transforming School Counseling* focuses on having school counselors become more interested in mental health problems, and less focused on individual academic needs of students (p. 437) (**F**).

39. With approval from its membership, ASCA has decided to withdraw from ACA and become a separate professional association (p. 441) (**F**).

40. If one becomes a licensed or certified school counselor in a state, one automatically becomes certified as a National Certified School Counselor (p. 4442) (**F**).

41. School counselors generally have privileged communication (p. 442) (**F**).

42. The Family Educational Rights and Privacy Act (The Buckley Amendment) assures the right of parents to have access to educational records, and probably counseling records (p. 443) (**T**).

43. The Hatch Amendment states that children cannot participate in research or experimental programs involving psychological examinations with parental informed consent (p. 443) (**T**).

44. School counselors must report suspected child abuse unless the principal says not to (p. 443) (**F**).

<u>Fill in The Blanks (questions 45-65)</u> (pp. 429-436)

Liste seven activities of the elementary, middle, and secondary school counselor

Elementary School Counselor	Middle School Counselor	Secondary School Counselor
45. ____________	52. ____________	59. ____________
46. ____________	53. ____________	60. ____________
47. ____________	54. ____________	61. ____________
48. ____________	55. ____________	62. ____________
49. ____________	56. ____________	63. ____________
50. ____________	57. ____________	64. ____________
51. ____________	58. ____________	65. ____________

<u>INFOTRAC KEY WORDS:</u> Comprehensive developmental counseling and guidance. Play therapy. Elementary school counseling. Middle school counseling. Secondary school counseling.

CHAPTER 17

COMMUNITY AGENCY COUNSELING

1. Which of the following is *not* true (p. 447)?
   a. CACREP accredits 60-credit-hour mental health counseling programs.
   b. CACREP accredits 48-credit-hour community agency counseling programs
   c. In many states, individuals who go through a non-accredited mental health *or* community agency counseling program can still get licensed as professional counselors
   d. None of the above (all are true)

2. The development of community agency/mental health counseling was impacted by all but which of the following (pp. 448-450)? (www)
   a. The emergence of psychoanalysis
   b. The spread of existential philosophy
   c. An increasingly humane attitude toward mental illness
   d. The vocational guidance movement
   e. The deinstitutionalization of tens of thousands of state mental hospital patients
   f. The awareness that most mental illness is the result of childhood abuse

3. The 1940s saw a number of events that greatly impacted upon the emergence of community agency/mental health counseling including (p. 449):
   a. success at shorter-term treatment approaches
   b. the establishment of the National Institute of Mental Health (NIMH)
   c. the passage of the National Mental Health Act
   d. the proliferation of a number of new, revolutionary approaches to counseling
   c. All but a
   f. All but b
   g. All but c
   h. All but d

4. The establishment of the Joint Commission on Mental Illness and Health did which of the following (p. 449)?
   a. Established community mental health centers
   b. Gave funding for research on the efficacy of treatment approaches
   c. Increased funding and services for mental health and mental illness
   d. All of the above

5. The Community Mental Health Centers Act of 1963 provided all but which of the following (p. 449)?
   a. Services for the elderly with dementia
   b. Short-term inpatient care
   c. Outpatient care
   d. Partial hospitalization
   e. Emergency services
   f. Consultation and education

6. This initiative, which was a product of the unrest of the 1960s, was instrumental to the establishment of a nationwide network of mental health agencies (p. 426).
   a. The National Institute of Mental Health Act
   c. The Joint Commission on Mental Illness and Health Act
   b. The National Mental Health Act
   d. The Community Mental Health Centers Act

7. Which legislative act contributed most to the deinstitutionalization of the mentally ill (p. 449)?
   a. The Supreme Court decision in O'Connor v. Donaldson
   b. The Tarasoff case
   c. Miller v. California, U. S. Supreme Court, 1973
   d. Passage of the Community Mental Health Centers Act

8. The ACA division which focuses on community agency/mental health counseling is (p. 450): (www)
   a. AMCD b. ASCA c. AMHCA d. CACA

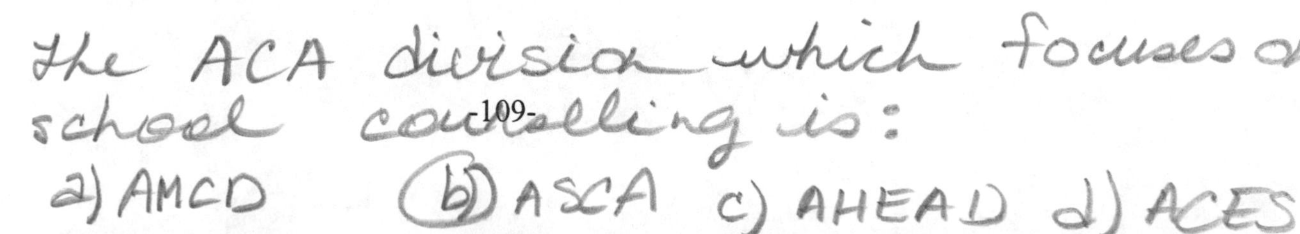

9. Three common places where you find rehabilitation counselors include (p. 452):
   a. VA hospitals, mental health centers, private agencies
   b. VA hospitals, vocational rehabilitation agencies, mental health centers
   c. mental health centers, employment services, vocational rehabilitation agencies
   d. VA hospitals, vocational rehabilitation agencies, private agencies

10. President Carter..... (p. 450)
   a. increased the focus on the importance of mental health treatment
   b. authorized the continuation and expansion of mental health services
   c. expanded the services of community mental health centers
   d. Two of the above
   e. All of the above

11. In which ways did block grants change the delivery of social services in the United States (p. 450)?
   a. It gave monetary aid to specific streets in communities.
   b. It resulted in a block of money given to the federal government earmarked for social services.
   c. It resulted in states being given a "block" of money for social service programs and resulted in less money for some services such as community mental health centers
   d. It gave sizable blocks of money to community mental health centers to broaden the services they provide

12. The proliferation of HMOs in the 1990s did which of the following (p. 450)? (www)
   a. Resulted in few services for mental health problems
   b. Increased the overseeing of mental health providers
   c. Decreased the cost of services for the public
   d. Increased the number of mental health providers
   e. Two of the above
   f. Three of the above

13. Which of the following are the five services provided by mental health centers at their inception and are now five of the twelve services offered (p. 449)?
   a. Short-term inpatient services, special services for the elderly, outpatient services, preinstitutional court screening, partial hospitalization (day treatment)
   b. Follow-up care for mental hospitals, emergency services, transitional care from mental hospitals, consultation and education, alcoholism services
   c. Special services for children, drug abuse services, short-term inpatient services, emergency services, consultation and education
   d. Short-term inpatient services, emergency services, consultation and education, outpatient services, drug abuse services
   e. Short-term inpatient services, emergency services, consultation and education, outpatient services, partial hospitalization (day treatment)

14. Generally, the primary function of the rehabilitation counselor is to (p. 452):
   a. provide long-term counseling
   b. develop treatment plans for insurance companies
   c. assess the client's disability and develop a plan to assist the client in obtaining a job, education, or career
   d. All of the above

15. The rehabilitation association affiliated with ACA is ___________, while a second association which some rehabilitation counselors join is __________ (p. 452).
   a. RAA; ARCA   b. ARCA; NRA   **c.** ARCA; NRCA   d. NRCA; ARCA

16. The association that accredits rehabilitation counseling programs is (p. 452):
   a. CACREP   d. a and b
   b. APA   e. a and c
   c. CORE   f. b and c

17. Many private practitioner counselors have expanded their repertoire of skills to include all but which of the following (p. 454)?
    - **a.** Forensic evaluations
    - b. Marital and divorce mediation
    - c. Educationally oriented workshops
    - d. Evaluations for adoptions and custody
    - e. Writing
    - f. Consultation to business and industry

18. One ACA division that focuses on gerontological issues is (p. 456):
    a. ACA b. AACA c. AAOP **d.** AADA

19. Which is not true about working with older persons (p. 455)?
    - a. A focus on prevention is important
    - b. A focus on treatment is important
    - c. Counselors often have to assist the elderly in dealing with negative stereotypes
    - d. Group counseling can be quite effective
    - **e.** The elderly are generally very open to counseling

20. In reference to substance abuse, which of the following is not true (p. 456)?
    - a. Approximately 45 million Americans binged on alcohol
    - b. Approximately 15 million Americans use illegal drugs and 12 million are heavy drinkers
    - c. Substance abuse has a major impact on the individual, families, and the society
    - **d.** Approximately 1 in 3 Americans are currently addicted to an illegal substance

21. The ACA division that focuses on chemical dependence is (p. 457):
    a. AACD b. AASA c. IACA **d.** IAAOC

22. Counselors who work in prisons find themselves in all but which of the following roles (p. 457)?
    - a. Counseling
    - b. Assessment
    - c. Crisis intervention
    - d. Consultation
    - e. Vocational training
    - f. Day-to-day adjustment problems
    - g. Making referrals
    - **h.** All of the above

23. The ACA division that focuses on working with people who are incarcerated is (p. 457):
    a. AAII b. AAP c. NAIPC **d.** IAAOC

24. Which of the following agencies has tended, until recently, to only hire social workers (p. 457)?
    - a. Employment agencies
    - **b.** Family service agencies
    - c. Youth service agencies
    - d. Residential treatment facilities
    - e. The military
    - f. Pastoral counseling centers

25. The ACA division which many counselors join who do marriage and family counseling is (p. 457):
    a. AMHCA b. AAMFT **c.** IAMFC d. ASCA

26. The ACA divisions which many counselors join who work in employment agencies are (p. 458):
    - a. NECA and NACC
    - b. ADVA and ECAA
    - c. ADVA and ECAA
    - **d.** NECA and NCDA

27. The ACA division which focuses on spiritual issues is (p. 459): (www)
    a. AASI **b.** ASERVIC c. C-AHEAD d. AASRC e. AAPC

28. Which is true about most licensed pastoral counselors (p. 459)?
    - **a.** They tend to integrate the basic precepts of their religious viewpoints with counseling theory
    - b. They tend to be dogmatic thinkers
    - c. There is no such thing as a licensed pastoral counselor
    - d. They are always ministers
    - e. Two of the above

29. A non ACA-affiliated association which some pastoral counselors join is (p. 459):
    a. AASI b. ASERVIC c. C-AHEAD d. AASRC **e.** AAPC

30. Which of the following was not identified as a major role of community agency/mental health counselors (pp. 459-460)?

a. Coordinator
b. Case Manager
c. Appraiser of client needs
d. Counselor
e. Consultant
f. Supervisor or supervisee
g. A professional who is accountable

31. The following would be an example of primary prevention (p. 461)

a. AIDS education
b. Stress management
c. Assertiveness training
d. Use of psychotropics
e. Two of the above
f. Three of the above
g. All of the above

32. Which of the following is *not* a principle that governs the ways in which counselors deliver services at agencies (p. 462)?

a. Respect for the client
b. Clients will progress in a facilitative environment
c. Counseling requires active participation upon the part of the client
d. Counseling should focus on strengths, not deficits
e. Counseling should help the client define realistic goals
f. Freedom to experiment with new techniques

33. Which is *not* true of HMOs (p. 450, 463):

a. HMOs refer only to their providers
b. HMOs are vigilante about overseeing the work of clinicians
c. HMOs require less paperwork as compared to traditional insurance companies
d. HMOs tend to provide fewer mental health services

34. Some drawbacks of DSM-IV-TR include all but which of the following (p. 464)?

a. It objectifies and depersonalizes the person
b. The labeling it provides leads to a self-fulfilling prophecy whereby the individual is seen as the diagnosis
c. It provides clinicians with a common language which tends to reinforce negative stereotyping of diagnoses
d. It creates artificial categories which we "buy into"
e. It provides few guidelines in making an accurate diagnosis

35. Which of the following is *not* a special issue in community agency/mental health counseling (pp. 463-464)? (www)

a. Changes in the health care delivery system
b. Deinstitutionalization of the mentally ill
c. The use of DSM-IV-TR
d. The use of psychotropic medications
e. The use of tertiary prevention techniques

36. Which of the following is *not* a multicultural issue faced by many community agency/mental health counselors (pp. 465-466)?

a. Most counseling theories are Western-based and might be dissonant with some minority cultures' values and attitudes
b. Some agency/mental health counselors may not have the sensitivity or the training necessary to work with minority clients
b. Many agency/mental health counselors have an ethnocentric world view
c. Many minority clients do not have access to effective counseling services because of the biases held by the majority culture
d. None of the above (all are issues)

37. Which of the following is the most frequently made complaint against Licensed Professional Counselors (p. 466)?
  a. Sexual relationship with a client
  b. Failure to report abuse
  c. Breach of confidentiality
  d. Inappropriate dual relationship
  e. Duty to warn

38. Of the complaints listed below, which represent the three types of ethical complaints made most frequently against counselors as noted by Neukrug, Milliken, & Walden (2001) (note: other complaints not included in this list) (p. 466)? (www)
  a. 1, 3, and 5
  b. 5, 6, 9
  c. 1, 2, 3
  d. 6, 7, 5
  e. 1, 6, 7
  f. 3, 4, 5

  1. Sexual relationship with a client
  2. Failure to report abuse
  3. Breach of confidentiality
  4. Sexual relationship with client
  5. Incompetence
  6. Practicing without a license or other misrepresentation
  7. Duty to warn
  8. Inappropriate fee assessment
  9. Inappropriate dual relationship

39. In most states, how many credit hours does it require to become a licensed professional counselor (p. 469)?
  a. 39 b. 48 **c.** 60 d. 90

True or False

40. An individual who receives a master's degree in counseling with an agency/mental health concentration can find employment at many agency settings and is generally eligible to apply for licensure as a professional counselor (p. 447) **(T)**.

41. The 1955 Mental Health Study Act resulted in the establishment of the Community Mental Health Centers Act (p. 449) **(F)**.

42. The Rehabilitation Act of 1973 ensured access to vocational rehabilitation services for the severely mentally or physically disabled and increased the need for rehabilitation counselors (p. 449) **(T)**.

43. Today, counseling programs that offer a degree in agency or mental health counseling comprise almost one-third of all graduate degrees in counseling (p. 450) **(F)**.

44. Mental health centers today still primarily rely on federal funding to maintain their existence (p. 451) **(F)**.

45. Recent statistics show that approximately 6 million Americans are in prison (p. 457) **(T)**.

46. Approximately 48 million adults and 5 million children in the United States have a disability (p. 451) **(T)**.

47. Rehabilitation counselors usually work in isolation due to their unique focus on disabilities (p. 452) **(F)**.

48. Rehabilitation counselors can become certified as Certified Rehabilitation Counselors (CRC) or as a National Certified Counselor (p. 452) **(T)**.

49. Most states now have licensure for counselors (p. 453) **(F)**.

50. Generally, with certification comes third-party reimbursement (p. 466) **(F)**.

51. Ironically, HMOs, EAPs, and PPOs, the very organizations that are making it increasingly difficult for private practitioners to work, are providing employment for other counselors (p. 455) **(T)**.

52. 1 out of every 10 Americans is in prison (p. 457) (F).

53. Interest in spiritual counseling seems to be waning (p. 458) (F).

54. Many individuals who do pastoral counseling are ministers and do not have a degree in counseling (p. 458) (T).

55. Because of the great number of places that you may find community agency/mental health counselors, their theoretical orientation may vary greatly (p. 462) (T).

56. A course in psychopathology or abnormal psychology has just recently become required by CACREP (p. 463) (F).

57. DSM-IV-TR offers 25 "culture-bound" syndromes that always represents deviant behaviors within cultures outside of the U. S. (p. 465) (F).

58. Misdiagnosis and misinterpretation of client problems are minor issues in the broad scheme of multicultural counseling (p. 465) (F).

59. The number of minority counselors has increased dramatically in the past ten years (p. 466) (F).

60. To become a Certified Clinical Mental Health Counselor (CCMHC) one must first become licensed as a professional counselor (p. 466) (F).

61. AMHCA's ethical guidelines have been rescinded in favor of ACAs guidelines (p. 467) (F).

(Questions 62-73) Fill in the Blanks (p. 451)
Today, mental health centers offer twelve services, and counselors can be found working in any of them. In the space provided, list as many of the services as you can:

62. ____________	68. ____________
63. ____________	69. ____________
64. ____________	70. ____________
65. ____________	71. ____________
66. ____________	72. ____________
67. ____________	73. ____________

(Questions 74-83) Fill in the Blank (pp. 450-460)
List eight places where you find agency/mental health counselors along with some of their major roles and functions:

	Places	Roles and functions
74.	____________	____________
75.	____________	____________
76.	____________	____________
77.	____________	____________
78.	____________	____________
79.	____________	____________
80.	____________	____________
81.	____________	____________
82.	____________	____________
83.	____________	____________

(Questions 84-95) Fill in the Blank (pp. 460-461)
In the space provided, place a short description of each of the roles of agency/mental health counselors listed below:

84. outreach worker........ ______________________________
85. broker........................ ______________________________
86. advocate.................... ______________________________
87. evaluator................... ______________________________
88. teacher/educator......... ______________________________
89. behavior changer........ ______________________________
90. mobilizer.................... ______________________________
91. community planner..... ______________________________
92. caregiver.................... ______________________________
93. data manager............. ______________________________
94. administrator............. ______________________________
95. clinical assistants........ ______________________________

INFOTRAC KEY WORDS: Community agency counseling. Managed care. Quality assurance. Ethical issues and mental health counselors.

CHAPTER 18

STUDENT AFFAIRS PRACTICE IN HIGHER EDUCATION

1. The earliest American colleges were (p. 473): (www)
   a. almost exclusively religiously affiliated
   b. had as their mission the development of *moral* men
   c. were some of the first state-affiliated colleges
   d. had as their mission the development of the whole person
   e. a and b
   f. b and c
   g. c and d

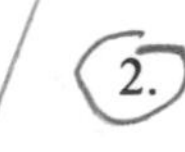

2. *In loco parentis*, during colonial times, was the concept that (p. 473):
   a. parents maintained control over their children, even when they're in college
   b. local parents would take on the responsibility of parenting children in away from home
   c. college faculty would take on the role of parenting and guiding students.
   d. local parents are crazy

3. The early part of the 19th century saw which of the following occur on college campuses (p. 473)?
   a. Increased parental involvement in campus affairs and student life
   b. Increased focus on the moral and religious development of students
   c. Decreased focus on the moral and religious development of students
   d. Increased role of faculty in the campus affairs and student life
   e. Two of the above

4. The end of the 19th century saw all but which of the following (p. 473)?
   a. The hiring of the first student affairs specialists
   b. The hiring of the first deans of students overseeing student affairs
   c. A renewed focus on the personal development of students
   d. A renewed religious focus and focus on the moral development of students

5. Which of the following was *not* one of the first student affairs associations (p. 474)?
   a. National Association of Women Deans and Counselors (NAWDAC)
   b. National Association of Student Personnel Administrators (NASPA)
   c. American College Counseling Association (ACCA)
   d. American College Personnel Association (ACPA)

6. Which of the following had an impact on the role that colleges played in the development of students at the beginning of the 20th century(p. 474)? (www)
   a. Emergence of psychoanalysis
   b. Testing and the vocational guidance movement
   c. The emergence of humanistic philosophies of counseling
   d. a and b
   e. a and c
   f. b and c

7. The 1940s saw a resurgence of student affairs practices which became known as which of the following (p. 474)?
   a. The Minnesota Point of View
   b. Client-centered counseling
   c. Trait and factor theory
   d. Student personnel point of view

8. During the 1960s the concept of *in loco parentis* became focused upon which of the following (p. 474)? (www)
   a. Parents maintaining control over their children, even when they're in college
   b. Local parents taking on the responsibility of parenting children in away from home
   c. College faculty taking on the role of parenting and guiding students.
   d. Students taking responsibility for themselves

9. Which of the following did *not* occur during the 1960s (p. 474)?
   a. Application of developmental theories
   b. Increasingly diverse campuses
   c. Decrease in federal aid as a result of the recession during the decade
   d. A rise in proactive interventions on centers (e.g., crisis centers, women's centers)
   e. None of the above (all of the above occurred)

10. The 1980s saw all but which of the following (p. 474)?
   a. Refinement of developmental theories
   b. Broadening of student affairs services
   d. Increase in federal laws affecting the practice of student affairs
   c. Cutbacks in funding
   e. None of the above (all of the above occurred)

11. The 1990s saw which of the following occur in student affairs practices (p. 474)?
   a. State and federal cutbacks to colleges
   b. Focus on the effectiveness of student services
   c. Reduction in the cost of offering services through consolidation and layoff
   d. All of the above

12. Which of the following is *not* a role of the student affairs practitioner as defined by Delworth and Hanson (1991) (pp. 479-480)?
   a. Campus ecology manager
   b. Systems analyzer
   c. Administrator
   d. Specialist
   e. Counselor

13. The essential elements that the administrator needs to focus upon to assure the successful functioning of students services include (p. 480):
   a. assessment, evaluation, programing, referrals, closure
   b. students, services and programs, structure, staff, sources
   c. intake, assessment, referral, evaluation
   d. assessment, analysis, implementation, evaluation, realignment

14. The administrator's main function relative to services and programs is (p. 480): (www)
   a. developing, implementing, and assessing their worthwhileness
   b. assuring faculty satisfaction
   c. assuring student satisfaction
   d. assuring the satisfaction of upper administration

15. In the role of counselor, which of the following is not important for the student affairs practitioner (p. 480)?
   a. A belief in the emotional, physical, spiritual, and interpersonal aspects of the student
   b. A belief that all students should have, at the minimum, a short-term counseling relationship to examine personal issues
   c. The importance of the affective domain in understanding the needs of students
   d. The importance of understanding developmental issues of students
   e. The importance of the personal characteristics of the helper

16. Which of the following is not an important role of the student affairs practitioner who is an educator (p. 481)?
   a. Advisor
   b. Mentor
   c. Curriculum builder/instructor
   d. Character builder
   e. Evaluator-assessor
   f. Scholar-researcher

17. The student affairs practitioner who is a campus ecology manger applies his or her roles in all but which of the following ways (p. 481)?
   a. Studying events and issues
   b. Creating an organizational framework
   c. Studying specific groups
   d. Examining contributions of each student services department
   e. All of the above

18. Which of the following is (are)a major student development theorist(s) (p. 482)? (www)
   a. Kegan
   b. Kohlberg
   c. Erikson
   d. Chickering
   e. Perry
   f. Two of the above
   g. Three of the above
   h. All but Kegan

19. Which of the following is *not* one of Chickering's seven vectors of student development (p. 483)?
   a. Achieving competence
   b. Managing emotions
   c. Developing autonomy
   d. Identifying with mentors
   e. Establishing identity
   f. Freeing interpersonal relationships
   g. Developing purpose
   h. Developing integrity

20. According to Chickering, managing one's sexuality is a major task of which of the following vectors (p. 483)?
   a. Achieving competence
   b. Managing emotions
   c. Developing autonomy
   e. Freeing interpersonal relationships
   f. Developing purpose
   g. Developing integrity

21. In Chickering's model, establishing identity has to do with understanding all but which of the following realms (p. 483)?
   a. Intellectual b. Physical c. Interpersonal competence d. Spiritual

22. Antonio is frequently finding himself unclear about the meaning of his life. He is likely dealing with which of Chickering's vectors (p. 457)?
   a. Achieving competence
   b. Managing emotions
   c. Developing autonomy
   e. Establishing identity
   f. Freeing interpersonal relationships
   g. Developing purpose
   h. Developing integrity

23. After years of reflection and struggle through college and graduate school about her identity and purpose in life, Jawanda now has a well-thought out internal belief system and feels good about herself. According to Chickering, Jawanda has a fairly well developed (p. 483):
   a. sense of self
   b. understanding of the world
   c. projective-reflective faith
   d. sense of integrity
   e. rational way of living

24. A student in an Introduction to Psychology class is pissed off at his professor because she refuses to take a stance on the etiology of mental illness. He is likely in which of Perry's stages (p. 484)?
   a. Dualism b. Transition c. Relativism d. Commitment to relativism

25. Tamara is an advanced graduate student in counseling. She used to adamantly believe that there were certain ethical guidelines that one must rigidly follow. She now struggles more with ethical decision making and feels torn up inside when considering some ethical decisions. She is likely in which of Perry's stages (p. 484)? (www)
   a. Dualism b. Transition c. Relativism d. Commitment to relativism

26. Which of the following does *not* lend itself toward barriers to academic excellence of underrepresented students (p. 485)?
   a. Differences in language
   b. Differences in ways of understanding the world
   c. General cultural differences
   d. Educational level of minorities

27. Today's concept of *In Loco Parentis* has generally been interpreted in which of the following ways (p. 485)?
   a. That faculty and staff have the responsibility to assist students who are away from home
   b. That the university should take on the role of parents *in absentia*
   c. That the university should protect the student's moral development
   d. That the university should protect students from harm

28. A main question that is being asked by student affairs practitioners as we move into the 21st century includes (p. 485)?
  a. Should student affairs solely support academics?
  b. Should student affairs support all aspects of the person's development?
  c. Should student affairs be a global unit of interacting offices, or separate offices?
  d. None of the above. Student affairs has "settled in" and currently has a sense of unified identity
  e. All of the above except "d"

29. Relative to multicultural issues, which of the following is *not* a main role of the student services practitioner (p. 486)?
  a. Addressing the student/faculty barrier
  b. Applying student development theory to minority students
  c. Implementing a cultural environment transitions model that embraces diversity
  d. Advocating, at the workplace, for controversial laws that support the education of minorities
  e. Assisting in the recruitment of staff that better reflects the diversity on campus

30. James is an advisor for the college. In the course of conversation with a student, he discovers that in one of the residence halls illegal drugs are being sold. What is James' responsibility (p. 487, 488)?
  a. James has responsibility to the client to keep the information confidential
  b. James has responsibility to the university to inform the proper authorities
  c. James had the responsibility to explain to his student the limits of confidentiality as a function of his role. James should act accordingly based on these limits
  d. James has no ethical or legal responsibility, strictly speaking

31. Which of the following is not an association for student affairs practitioners (p. 487)?
  a. ASAA b. NASPA c. ACPA d. NAWDC e. NCDA f. ACCA

32. The Buckley Amendment does which of the following (p. 489)?
  a. Assures the rights of the public to view publications of the university as a contract
  b. Assures that the civil rights of all students is not violated
  c. Assures that individuals cannot defame others in written or oral materials
  d. Assures all individuals the right to inspect their educational records

33. In the local school newspaper, the editor has made some unsubstantiated statements that seriously impugn the character of a faculty member. The faculty member has threatened to sue. Chances are (p. 488):
  a. he has no case. Freedom of speech is guaranteed by the First Amendment to the constitution
  b. he cannot sue. Faculty have no right to sue students at a university
  c. he can sue and will likely win. Past cases assure that the faculty member cannot be slandered by a school newspaper
  d. he may have a case. Increasingly, universities are needing to monitor materials that may defame others or which may limit their civil rights

True or False

34. The earliest American colleges had faculty take on most of the roles in which we now find student development specialists (p. 473) **(T)**.

35. The latter part of the 19th century saw a movement away from focusing on the personal development of students (p. 473) **(F)**.

36. The first deans of students were hired at the end of 18th century (p. 473) **(F)**.

37. Social problems during the depression led to an increase in student affairs professionals (p. 474) **(F)**.

38. Student services administrators, as a function of their role, must make decisions for the needs of the university as opposed to the needs of the student (p. 480) **(F)**.

39. A student services administrator needs to assure that the lines of communications within and between services offered are clear (p. 480) **(T)**.

40. Although not all student affairs practitioners do counseling, they all embrace the ideals and values of counselors (p. 480) (**T**).

41. The student affairs practitioner who is an educator often will assist faculty in the development of curricula that will have a positive impact on the student (p. 481) (**T**).

42. Because the student affairs practitioner who is an advisor meets with students for relatively short periods of time, their interventions must not include an analysis of time-consuming developmental concerns (p. 481) (**F**).

43. Although the needs of varying groups on campuses differ, the types of interventions that are made are the same (p. 482) (**F**).

44. A systemic understanding of organizational structure is necessary if the student affairs practitioner who is an ecology manager is to work effectively (pp. 481-482) (**T**).

45. The role of manager of campus ecology dates back to the functions and roles of the early Deans of Student Services (pp. 481-482) (**F**).

46. In Chickering's model, to develop in higher vectors, one has to have become fully developed in lower vectors (p. 483) (**F**).

47. Perry believed that changes in intellectual and ethical development were a function of age, education, and experience and thus, there was little one can do to move a person to higher-level thinking (pp. 483-484) (**F**).

48. Few adults ever meet Perry's highest stage of commitment in relativism (p. 484) (**T**).

49. As we move into the 21st century, a unifying philosophy of student affairs appears to be coalescing (p. 486) (**F**).

50. The academic vice-president at a state university insists on using the term *Christmas vacation* instead of holiday vacation. The student affairs practitioner has a responsibility to explain to the vice-president that the use of this term is offensive to some (p. 487) (**T**).

51. The Tarasoff rule suggests that counselors in college counseling settings have the right to confidentiality under all circumstances (p. 487) (**F**).

52. A university can potentially be held libel if harm comes to a student, such as the case of harm as the result of alcohol abuse (p. 488) (**T**).

53. Generally, parents *do not have the rights* to their students records at the post-secondary level (p. 489) (**T**).

(Questions 54-63) Fill in the Blank (pp. 475-482)

List eight places where you find student affairs practitioners along with some of their major roles and functions:

	Places	Roles and functions
54.	____________	____________
55.	____________	____________
56.	____________	____________
57.	____________	____________
58.	____________	____________
59.	____________	____________
60.	____________	____________
61.	____________	____________
62.	____________	____________
63.	____________	____________

INFOTRAC KEY WORDS: College student development. Theories of college student development. Ethics and college counseling..

CHAPTER 19

A LOOK TOWARD THE FUTURE

1. Which of the following may be some of the diseases for which we might find a genetic link (p. 494)?
   a. Heart Disease
   b. Cancer
   c. Schizophrenia
   d. Bipolar Disorder
   e. Depression
   f. Anxiety
   <u>g.</u> All of The Above

2. A counselor who treated a client without knowledge of the effectiveness of medications would be (p. 494): (www)
   a. involved in holistic health
   b. practicing the mind-body connection
   c. considering alternative options
   <u>d.</u> practicing incompetence
   e. None of the above

3. Evidence suggests that meditation and other mind-altering experiences can do which of the following (p. 495)?
   a. Reduce stress
   b. Can alleviate stress-related illnesses
   c. Be helpful in recovery from mental health problems
   d. a and b
   e. b and c
   <u>f.</u> All of the above

4. In reference to mental health treatment, health insurance companies today (p. 495): (www)
   a. offer fewer services for mental health treatment
   b. want stricter documentation of the services they provide
   c. want evidence that treatment is progressing
   d. have an expectation that treatment will be brief
   e. a and b
   f. b and c
   <u>g.</u> All of the above

5. For the agency/mental health counselor, some results of the stricter overseeing of mental health providers and other changes in the health care system may be all but which of the following (p. 496)?
   a. Offering some services for free or reduced cost
   b. Terminating services early
   c. Becoming knowledgeable about brief-treatment approaches
   d. Two of the above
   <u>e.</u> All of the above

6. Currently, what is the approximate percentage of homes with a computer (p. 496)?
   a. 25% <u>b.</u> 61% c. 75% d. 90% e. 95%

7. Relative to counseling on-line, which is true (p.)?
   a. Counseling on-line is unethical
   b. Counselors are acting illegal if they counsel on-line
   <u>c.</u> If counseling on-line, counselors need to follow ACAs Ethical Guidelines for Internet On-line Counseling
   d. a and b

8. Counseling on the Internet (p. 496):
   a. May offer many advantages
   b. May be riddled with problems
   c. Should never be done
   <u>d.</u> a and b

9. What should not be included in a portfolio (p. 496)?
   a. Transcipts
   b. Statement of your philosophy
   c. Papers you have written
   d. Workshops presented
   e. Any item that positively highlights your abilities
   f. None of the above (all can be included)

10. Some professional publications one might look in to respond to an ad for a job include all but which of the following (p. 499)?
   a. Chronicle of Counselor Education
   b. Counseling Today
   c. APA Monitor
   d. Counseling Today
   e. Chronicle of Higher Education

11. Criticism(s) of CACREP accreditation include(s) which of the following (p. 501)? (www)
   a. Small programs will have difficulty becoming accredited
   b. Creativity is thwarted
   c. Students will have few programs to which they may apply
   d. Standards are compromised
   e. a and b
   f. b and c
   g. Three of the above

12. One of the major researchers on the effects of stress on the person is (p. 502):
   a. Jacob Stressor
   b. Leonard Silverman
   c. Cecil Myaber
   d. Hans Selye

13. Which divisions of ACA have asked their members to vote on disaffiliation (p. 502)?
   a. ACPA and ACES
   b. AMHCA and ASCA
   c. ASCA and ACES
   d. ACES and AMHCA
   e. ACPA and AMHCA
   f. ACPA and ASCA

14. As identified throughout Chapter 19, which of the following is *not* likely to be a major issue in the next millennium)?
   a. Changes in specialty areas in counseling
   b. Medical breakthroughs
   c. Healthcare delivery systems
   d. Stress and burnout
   e. Computers and the information superhighway
   f. Multicultural issues
   g. Standards in the profession

15. Which is not a domain of Myers, Sweeny, and Witmer's (2000) Wheel of Wellness (pp. 502-503)?
   a. Spirituality
   b. Work and leisure
   c. Friendship
   d. Stress
   e. Love
   f. Self-direction

16. Credentialing is important to(p. 501): (www)
   a. helping counselors obtain jobs
   b. obtaining 3rd party payments
   c. demonstrating a high standards of care
   d. all of the above

17. Which of the following is not a standard of care we are likely to see highlighted in the coming years (p.501)? (www)
   a. increased use of professional disclosure statements
   b. more formative and summative evaluations
   c. focus on ethical, professional, and multicultural issues
   d. increased used of long-term treatment modalities to assure quality care
   e. increased focus on good case note taking and treatment planning

True or False

18. Legal issues relative to genetic counseling are out of the realm of counselor competence and should be left to lawyers (p. 493). (**F**)

19. Counselors are trying to obtain the legal right to prescribe medications (p. 484). (**F**)

20. Research on the connection between physical and emotional states shows that one's mental state is closely related to one's physical state (p. 495). (**T**)

21. The cost of mental health services has been slowly declining (p. 495). (**F**)

22. One result of the expanded use of HMOs is the increased in referrals they make to mental health services as compared to traditional insurance companies (p. 495). (**F**)

23. The first PCs were sold in the 1960s (p. 496). (**F**)

24. Although responding to ads in the newspaper is generally not the best way to find a job, it is one more method worth trying (p. 500) (**T**).

25. The purpose of informational interviews, it to obtain a job (p. 499) (**F**).

26. Resumes should not be more than one or two pages long (p. 497). (**F**)

27. Being denied acceptance into a graduate program or not obtaining a desired job is an indication that one should seek a new career direction in life (p. 500) (**F**).

28. Most counseling students are not content with the training they have obtained in multicultural counseling (p. 500). (**T**)

29. Stress is an adaptive response to a changing situation (p. 502) (**F**).

30. Today, about 75% of counseling programs are CACREP-accredited (p. 501) (**F**)

31. Today, ACA is an organization that changes with the times (p. 502) (**T**)

(Questions 32 - 38) Fill in the Blank

List seven ways that counselors now use computers (pp. 496)

32. ______________________________
33. ______________________________
34. ______________________________
35. ______________________________
36. ______________________________
37. ______________________________
38. ______________________________

(Questions 39 - 52) Fill in the Blanks

List seven advantages and seven drawbacks of counseling on the Internet (p. 497).

Advantages	Drawbacks
39. ________________	46. ________________
40. ________________	47. ________________
41. ________________	48. ________________
42. ________________	49. ________________
43. ________________	50. ________________
44. ________________	51. ________________
45. ________________	52. ________________

(Questions 53 - 66) Fill in the Blanks (p. 496-500).

List as many points that one should consider when applying to graduate school:

53. ______________ 60. ______________
54. ______________ 61. ______________
55. ______________ 62. ______________
56. ______________ 63. ______________
57. ______________ 64. ______________
58. ______________ 65. ______________
59. ______________ 66.. ______________

(Questions 67 - 74) Fill in the Blanks (pp. 496-500)
Below are a number of points to consider when applying to graduate school. For each listed, describe what it is and write in some ways that one can optimize the application process.

67. Meeting deadlines______________
68. Completing forms______________
69. Taking a cognitive ability test______________
70. Writing an essay______________ ______________
71. Interviewing______________
72. Submitting a resume______________
73. Preparing a portfolio______________
74. Being admitted, being denied______________

(Questions 75 - 81) Fill in the Blanks (p. 499-500)
In the space provided, fill in six methods one might use at finding a job.

75. ______________
76. ______________
77. ______________
78. ______________
79. ______________
80. ______________
81. ______________

(Questions 82 - 89) Fill in the Blank (p. 501)
List eight standards of care that counselors should increasingly be concerned about.

1. ______________
2. ______________
3. ______________
4. ______________
5. ______________
6. ______________
7. ______________
8. ______________

(Questions 90 - 96) Fill in the Blank (p. 481)
List six ways of keeping oneself alive and reducing stress.

9. ______________
10. ______________
11. ______________
12. ______________
13. ______________
14. ______________

Short Essays (pp. 502-503)

15. Discuss the importance of intermingling with people of different cultures.

INFOTRAC KEY WORDS: Stress. Burnout. Technology and counseling. Quality assurance. Trends in counseling. Standards of care.

SYLLABUS
PRINCIPLES OF COUNSELING

INSTRUCTOR: Edward Neukrug, Ed.D.

COURSE NUMBER: Coun 601

COURSE TITLE: Principles of Counseling

COURSE DESCRIPTION: To obtain an overview of theory, practice, methods, basic principles, and concepts used in educational settings and community agencies by counselors.

PURPOSE OF COURSE: The purpose of this course is to have students gain an overview of the counseling profession through readings, class discussion, experiential activities and site visits. By the end of the course students will have a clear understanding of what it entails to be a counselor and be able to distinguish a counselor from related mental health professions. In addition, students will begin to see themselves as having taken their first step toward being a professional counselor. Finally, students will be able to make an informed decision regarding the likelihood that the counseling profession is their best path.

COURSE OBJECTIVES:

1. To begin to define the terms guidance, counseling, and psychotherapy: Variations on the same theme?

2. To compare and contrast counselors with psychologists, psychiatrists, social workers, psychotherapists, and psychiatric nurses.

3. To distinguish the various counseling specialty areas of school counseling, mental health counseling, community counseling, counseling in student affairs practices, rehabilitation counseling, gerontological counseling, and marriage and family counseling.

4. The examine and discuss the characteristics of the effective counselor including empathy, genuineness, acceptance, open-mindedness, internality, competence, being mentally healthy, and being capable of building alliances.

5. To examine the historical roots of counseling, and examine its relationship to the historical roots of psychology, psychiatry, and social work.

6. To learn about three standards in the profession: ethics, accreditation, and credentialing.

7. To review counseling theories, particularly four conceptual approaches to counseling: psychodynamic, existential-humanistic, behavioral, cognitive, and some theories that are associated with them. To understand eclecticism (theoretical integrative approach) and examine brief-treatment and solution-focused therapies.

8. To review the basics to building and implementing a counseling relationship, including the office environment, basic and advanced counseling skills, case conceptualization, and record keeping.

9. To understand general systems theory and how it applies to family counseling, group counseling, consultation, supervision, and all living systems.

10. To review basic principles to family counseling and examine the following models of family therapy: structural, strategic, communication, multigenerational, experiential, psychodynamic, and behavioral.

11. To review the history of group work, understand group dynamics and group process, and distinguish among the following groups: self-help groups, task groups, psychoeducational groups, counseling groups, and group therapy.

12. To review the history of consultation, understand the consulting process, and be able to distinguish among the following models and types of consultation: consultant centered, system centered, person-centered, learning theory, gestalt, psychoanalytic, and chaos.

13. To define supervision, examine its relationship to consultation, and be able to distinguish among the following types of supervision: developmental, orientation-specific, and integrated.

14. To review physical and psychosocial developmental concepts; the cognitive and moral development theories of Piaget, Kohlberg, and Gilligan; the adult cognitive development theories of Kegan and Perry; the lifespan development theories of Erickson and Levinson; and the faith development theory of Fowler.

15. To study the etiology of abnormal development as presented by geneticists and biologists, Freud, existential-humanistic, and learning theorists.

16. To review the Diagnostic and Statistical Manual-IV-TR.

17. To understand the purpose and usage of psychotropic medication.

18. To review the history of career development, basic definitions related to the career development process, and to understand the following theories of career development: trait-and-factor, Holland's personality theory, Roe's psychodynamic theory, Super's lifespan theory, cognitive theory, and others. To understand the relationship between occupational information and career counseling.

19. To understand the difference between testing and assessment, the purposes of testing, different kinds of tests that are used, basic tests statistics, and qualities that make a good test, such as validity, reliability, cross-cultural fairness, and practicality.

20. To understand the purpose of research and review the different kinds of quantitative and qualitative research approaches. To review the purpose and use of evaluation and compare and contrast it to research.

21. To learn about diversity in the United States, review problems of cross-cultural counseling such as the misdiagnosis of minority clients, review minority and white identity models, and examine how to counsel individuals from select cultural groups in the United States.

22. To review the history, roles and functions, and settings where you find school counselors, community agency/mental health counselors, and student affairs practice in higher education counselors.

23. To learn how to choose and apply to graduate school, how to find a job in the counseling profession, and the future outlook for jobs in the counseling profession.

24. To examine trends in the future including medical breakthroughs, the changing nature of therapeutic practice, the use of computers and the information superhighway, and the affects of stress, cynicism, and burnout.

25. To examine how multicultural issues, ethical issues, and professional issues permeate all of what we do as a professional.

26. To become familiar with local, state, and national organizations, agencies, educational settings, and resources relevant to the counseling profession.

COURSE REQUIREMENTS:

1. Text readings as assigned.
2. Paper: An eight to ten page paper, using APA referencing, on any aspect of the counseling profession related to the student's area of concentration (e.g., school, agency, college). The paper should include a minimum of twelve journal references.
3. Involvement in experiential exercises.
4. Midterm and Final.
5. Group Projects:

   a. *Outline and presentation:* Your group is asked to outline the chapter in the book that highlights your specialty area (school, agency, or college) and present the information in the chapter to the class in a creative and exciting manner.

   b. *Site visit:* Within your emphasis area, you will be asked to break down into groups of three to five students and with your group, visit and analyze counseling at an elementary, middle or secondary school; mental health agency; or college. Outlines for you review will be distributed in class (note: these outlines are in th workbook: *Experiencing the world of the counselor: A workbook for counselor educators and students*).

ACCOMMODATING STUDENTS WITH SPECIAL LEARNING NEEDS:

In accordance with university policy, a student who wishes to receive some instructional accommodation, because of a documented sensory and/or learning disability, should meet with the instructor to discuss this accommodation.

ATTENDANCE:

Although attendance and participation are not mandatory, as a graduate course, it is expected that students will embrace the learning process through their attendance and participation.

GRADING:

Point Spread for Grade Determination

92.1	to	100	= A		78	to	79.9	= B-
90	to	92	= A-		75	to	77.9	= C+
85	to	89.9	= B+		70	to	74.9	= C
80	to	84.9	= B		68	to	69.9	= C-

20% - Midterm and Final — 20% - Paper
20% - Group presentation — 20% - Agency Visit Paper

HONORS PLEDGE:

"I pledge to support the honor system of Old Dominion University. I will refrain from any form of academic dishonest or deception, such as cheating or plagiarism. I am aware that as a member of the academic community, it is my responsibility to turn in all suspected violators of the honor system. I will report to Honor Council hearings if summoned." By attending Old Dominion University you have accepted the responsibility to abide by this code. This is an institutional policy approved by the Board of Visitors.

CLASS REFERENCES:

Neukrug, E. S. (2003). *The world of the counselor: An introduction to the counseling profession* (2nd ed.). Pacific Grove, CA: Brooks/Cole.

Neukrug, E. S. (2003). *Experiencing the world of the counselor: A workbook for counselor educators and students*. Pacific Grove, CA: Brooks/Cole.

OFFICE HOURS: Office hours are by appointment. Dr. Neukrug can be reached at 683-3221 or at eneukrug@odu.edu.

COURSE SEQUENCING: This course is typically the first course taken in the counseling program. For students considering the counseling profession, this is one of two courses that can be taken in the program without having been admitted into the program. This course is a prerequisite for all courses except Counseling Skills (Coun 633), Testing and Individual Appraisal (Coun 645), and Counseling Theories (Coun 650) for which it is a corequisite.

COURSE CONTENT:

	Weeks
Section I: Professional Orientation:	1 & 2
Chapter 1: The Counselor's Identity: What, Who, and How?	
Chapter 2: A History of the Counseling Profession	
Chapter 3: Standards in the Profession: Ethics, Accreditation, and Credentialing	
Section II: The Helping Relationship I: Theory and Skills:	3 & 4
Chapter 4: Individual Approaches to Counseling	
Chapter 5: Counseling Skills	
Section III: The Helping Relationship II: The Counselor Working in Systems	5 & 6
Chapter 6: Family Counseling	
Chapter 7: Group Work	
Chapter 8: Consultation and Supervision	
Midterm:	7
Section IV: Development of the Person:	8 & 9
Chapter 9: Development Across the Lifespan	
Chapter 10: Abnormal Development, Diagnosis, and Psychopathology	
Chapter 11: Career Development: The Counselor and the World of Work	
Section V: Research, Program Evaluation, and Appraisal:	10 & 11
Chapter 12: Testing and Assessment	
Chapter 13: Research and Evaluation	
Section VI: Social and Cultural Foundations in Counseling:	12 & 13
Chapter 14: Theory and Concepts to Multicultural Counseling	
Chapter 15: Knowledge and Skills of Multicultural Counseling.	
Section VII: Your Future in the Counseling Profession: Choosing a Specialty Area, Finding a Job, and Trends in the Future.	14 & 15
Chapter 16: School Counseling	
Chapter 17: Community Agency Counseling	
Chapter 18: Student Affairs Practice in Higher Education	
Chapter 19: A Look Toward the Future	
Final	16

SECTION AND CHAPTER OVERHEADS

SECTION I: PROFESSIONAL ORIENTATION

Chapter 1: The Counselor's Identity: What, Who, and How?

Defining Guidance, Counseling, and Psychotherapy: Variations on Same Theme?

Comparison of Mental Health Professionals

- Counselors
  - School Counselors
  - Mental Health/agency Counselors
  - College Counselors
  - Rehabilitation Counselors
  - Marriage, Couple, and Family Counselors
  - Others?

- Psychologists
  - Clinical Psychologists
  - School Psychologists
  - Counseling Psychologists

- ✲ Psychiatrists
- ✲ Social Workers
- ✲ Psychiatric Nurses
- ✲ Psychoanalysts

<u>Professional Associations</u>

- ✲ Beneifits of
- ✲ The Associations

<u>Names of Associations</u>

- ✲ ACA - American Counseling Association
- ✲ APA - American Psychological Association
- ✲ APA - American Psychiatric Association

<u>Names of Associations (Cont'd)</u>

- ✲ NASW - National Association of Social Workers
- ✲ APNA - American Psychiatric Nurses Assoc.
- ✲ AAMFT - American Association of Marriage & Family Therapists
- ✲ NOHSE - National Organization for Human Service Education

Characteristics of the Effective Helper

- Empathy
- Genuineness
- Open-mindedness
- Relationship Building
- Mindfulness (Internality)
- Acceptance
- Psychological Adjustment
- Competence

The Effective Counselor: A Constructivist Developmental Perspective

Multicultural Issues

- The Helping Professions' Responsibility to Minority Clients
- A Call to the Profession: Inclusion of Multiculturalism

Ethical, Professional, and Legal Issues

- Knowing Who We Are and Our Relationship to Other Professionals
- Impaired Mental Health Professionals

The Counselor in Process: Personal Therapy and Related Growth Experiences

Chapter 2

A History of the Counseling Profession

Understanding The Human Condition From Early Antiquity to The Present

- Shamans
- Other early history?

A Brief History of Related Helping Professions

- Social work
- Psychology
- Psychiatry
- Influence of Social Work, Psychology, and Psychiatry on Counseling

Early History of the Counseling Profession

- Social Reform Movement
- Vocational Guidance
- Testing Movement
- Psychoanalysis & Development of Psychotherapy

Modern Day Counseling: Early Beginnings

- Early Vocational Guidance, First Guidance Counselors
- Expansion of the Testing Movement
- Spread of Psychotherapy

Modern Day Counseling

- 1950s: Emergence, Expansion, Diversification
- 1960s: Increased Diversification
- 1970s: Continued Proliferation
- 1980-2000: Recent Changes in the Field
- 2000 and Beyond: The New Millennium

Do We Have to Memorize All Those Names?

Summary of Important Historical Events

Multicultural Issues:

- ✲ Learning from the Past, Moving Toward the Future
- ✲ Reasons why Change has been Slow
- ✲ AMCD

Ethical, Professional, and Legal Issues in Counseling

- ✲ Ethical Guidelines: A Short but Important History

The Counselor in Process: Looking Back, Looking Ahead, and Paradigm Shifts

Chapter 3:
Standards in the Profession :Ethics, Accreditation, and Credentialing

Ethics

- Defining Values, Ethics, Morality, and Their Relationship to the Law

- What Is Ethically Correct Behavior?

- Development of/need for Ethical Codes
  - Brief Overview of Aca Ethical Standards
  - Related Ethical Codes and Standards

- Resolving Ethical Dilemmas
  - Decision-making Models
  - A Developmental Perspective

- Ethical Complaints and Violations
  - Problem Areas for Counselors
  - Reporting Ethical Violations

- Legal Issues Related to Ethical Violations
  - Civil and Criminal Liability
  - Role of Ethical Codes in Lawsuits
  - Malpractice Insurance and Counseling

<u>Accreditation</u>

- History and Development of Preparation Standards

- CACREP
  - A Short History of CACREP
  - Overview of the CACREP Standards

- Other accreditation bodies

<u>Credentialing</u>

- Registration
- Certification
- Licensure

- Credentialing in Related Helping Professions
  - Social Work
  - Psychologist
  - Marriage and Family Therapy
  - Psychiatry
  - Psychiatric Nurse

- History and Current Status of Credentialing for Counselors
  - Certified Rehabilitation Counselor
  - National Counselor Certification
  - Speciality Certifications in Counseling: Addictions, School, Approved Clinical Supervisor, Marriage and Family
  - Licensed Professional Counselors

<u>Multicultural Issues: How Standards Address Multicultural Counseling</u>

- Inclusion of Multicultural Issues
  - ACAs Ethical Standards,
  - Credentialing Exams

Multiculturla Issues (Cont'd)

* Accreditation Standards
* Multicultural Counseling Competencies

Ethical, Professional, and Legal Issues

* Unified Ethical Standards
* Counseling On-Line
* Promoting Professionalism

The Counselor in Process: Commitment to Professionalism

SECTION II: THE HELPING RELATIONSHIP I: THEORY AND SKILLS

Chapter 4: Individual Approaches to Counseling

Why Have a Counseling Theory?

Four Conceptual Orientations & Aligned Theories

- Psychodynamic Approaches
- Existential-Humanistic Approaches
- Behavioral Approaches
- Cognitive Approaches

Psychodynamic Approaches

- Early Beginnings and View of Human Nature
- Freud's psychoanalysis
  - Instincts
  - Structure of personality

- Psychosexual stages of development
- Ego Defense Mechanisms
- Techniques
- The therapeutic relationship

- Other Psychodynamic Approaches
  - Jung's Analytical Psychology
  - Adlerian Therapy
  - Mahler's Object-Relations Theory

<u>Existential-Humanistic Approaches</u>

- Early Beginnings and View of Human Nature
- Carl Rogers & Person-centered counseling
  - "Necessary & sufficient conditions"
  - "Techniques:"
    - Congruence/genuineness
    - Unconditional positive regard
    - Empathic understanding
  - The Therapeutic Relationship

Other Existential-Humanistic Approaches

- Gestalt Therapy (Perls)
- Existential Therapy

Behavioral Approaches

- Early beginnings and view of human nature
- Approaches: 1) Classical conditioning, 2) Operant conditioning, 3) Modeling

- Modern Behaviorism
  - Therapeutic stages
  - Techniques
    - Modeling
    - Operant conditioning
    - Relaxation exercises & systematic desensitization
    - Self-management
    - Flooding & implosion
  - The Therapeutic Relationship

Other Behavioral Approaches

- ✲ Lazarus' Multimodal Therapy (BASIC ID)
- ✲ Glasser's Reality Therapy & Choice Theory

Cognitive Approaches

- ✲ Defining Cognitive Therapy and View of human nature

Cognitive Approaches

- ✲ Rational-emotive-behavior Therapy
- ✲ Ellis' View of Human Nature
- ✲ ABCs of Personality Formation
- ✲ Techniques
    - ✲ Cognitive Homework
    - ✲ Bibliotherapy
    - ✲ Role-playing
    - ✲ Shame-attacking Exercises
    - ✲ Imagery Exercises
    - ✲ Behavioral Techniques
    - ✲ Emotive Techniques
- ✲ The Therapeutic Relationship

Other Cognitive Approaches

- Beck's Cognitive Therapy
- Mahoney's Constructivism

Current Theoretical Trends

- Integrative Approaches (Eclecticism)
    - Stages: Chaos, Coalescence, Theoretical Integration, Metatheory
- Brief therapies
    - Garfield's Stage Model
    - Solution-focused Therapy

Multicultural Issues Biases in Counseling Theory

- Psychodynamic Approach
- Existential-Humanistic Approach
- Behavioral Approach
- Cognitive Approach
- Brief-treatment Approaches

Ethical, Professional, & Legal Issues The Counseling Relationship

- Respecting the welfare of the client
- Respecting diversity
- Clients' rights
- Dual relationships
- Termination & referral
- Respect for the client's right to confidentiality
- Exceptions to confidentiality
- Privileged communication v. confidentiality

The Counselor in Process: Embracing a Theory but Open to Change

Chapter 5
Counseling Skills

The Counseling Environment

- ✲ The Office
- ✲ Nonverbal Behavior
- ✲ Counselor Qualities to Embrace/counselor Qualities to Avoid

Counseling Skills

- ✲ Foundational Skills: 1) Listening, 2) Empathy, 3) Silence

Commonly-used Skills

Questions

1) Purpose of Questions
2) Open v. closed
3) Direct v. indirect
4) Why questions
5) Problems with Questions

- ✲ Counselor Self-disclosure (Commonly used Skills Cont'd)
  - ✲ Content Self-disclosure
  - ✲ Process Self-disclosure

- Modeling (Commonly-used Skills Cont'd)
    - Circuitous Modeling
    - Intentional modeling

- Confrontation: Challenge with Support
    - Confronting Client Discrepancies

- Interpretation

Skills to Use Cautiously

- Encouragement, Affirmation, and Self-esteem Building
- Offering Alternatives, Information Giving, and Advice Giving

Advanced and Specialized Skills

Case Conceptualization

- Conceptualizing Client Problems
- IPH: Inverted Pyramid Heuristic

Stages of the Counseling Relationship

1. Rapport & trust building
2. Problem identification
3. Deepening understanding & goal setting
4. Work
5. Closure
6. Follow-up

Case Notes & Record Keeping

- Writing case notes
- Security of record keeping

Multicultural Issue: Applying Skills Cross-Culturally

Ethical, Professional, and Legal Issues

- Client's rights to records
- Confidentiality/Privileged communication
  - Jaffe v. Redmond

The Counselor in Process: The Developmental Nature of Counseling Skills

SECTION III: THE HELPING RELATIONSHIP II: THE COUNSELOR WORKING IN SYSTEMS

Chapter 6: Family Counseling

A Brief History

General Systems Theory

- Boundaries and Information Flow in Family Systems

Dysfunctional and Healthy Families

Models of Family Therapy

- Structural Family Therapy
  - Rules
  - Boundaries
  - Structure and Hierarchy
  - Stress
  - Joining
  - Restructuring

Models of Family Therapy (Cont'd)

- Strategic Family Therapy (Models of Family Therapy Cont'd)
  - Haley's Stages of Strategic Therapy
  - Directives

- Communication Approaches: Satir

- Multigenerational Approaches
  - Boszormenyi-nagy
  - Bowen
  - Use of Genogram

- Experiential Family Therapy: Whitaker

- Psychodynamic Approaches: Skynner and Ackerman

- Behavioral Family Therapy

Multicultural Issue: Points to Consider When Working with Minority Families

Ethical, Professional, & Legal Issues in Family Counseling

- Withholding Treatment in Order to See the Whole Family
- Informed Consent
- Confidentiality
- Dual Relationships
- Individual or Family Therapy?
- Professional Associations: AAMFT, IAMFC
- Accreditation & Credentialing in Family Counseling
- Testifying Against a Family Member
- Insurance Fraud

Counselor in Process: Understanding Our Clients Family, Understanding Our Family

Chapter 7
Group Work

Groups: A Systemic Perspective

Why Have Groups?

- Advantages and Disadvantages

History of Group Counseling

- Early History
- Emergence of Modern-day Groups
- Groups Become Faddish
- Recent Trends

Defining Modern-day Groups

- Self-help Groups
- Task Groups
- Psychoeducational Groups
- Comparing Psychoeducational, Counseling, and Therapy Groups
- Counseling Groups
- Group Therapy

Use of Theory in Group Work

- Psychoanalytic Group Therapy
- Behavioral Group Therapy
- Rational-emotive-behavior Group Therapy
- Person-centered Group Counseling

Group Process

- Preparing for the Group
    - Getting Members
    - Group Composition
    - Closed or Open Group
    - Size of Group
    - Duration of Meetings
    - Frequency of Meetings
    - Securing an Appropriate Space

- ✲ Stages of Group Development
  1) Pregroup Stage
  2) Initial Stage
  3) Transition Stage
  4) Work Stage
  5) Closure Stage

<u>Group Leadership Styles</u>

<u>Multicultural Issues</u>

- ✲ Principles for Diversity-competent Group Workers
- ✲ The Group as a Microcosm of Society
- ✲ Group Leader/member Cultural Differences

<u>Ethical, Professional, & Legal Issues in Group Counseling</u>

- ✲ Informed Consent
- ✲ Confidentiality
- ✲ Group vs. Individual Counseling
- ✲ Professional Associations
- ✲ Confidentiality & Third-party Rule

<u>The Counselor in Process: Allowing Groups to Unravel Naturally</u>

Chapter 8
Consultation and Supervision

Consultation

- ✲ Defining Consultation

- ✲ Brief History of Consultation
  - ✲ The Beginning
  - ✲ Expansion of Models of Consultation
  - ✲ Recent Trends in Consultation
    - ✲ A Systemic Perspective
    - ✲ A Developmental and Preventive Perspective

Models of Consultation

1) System-centered Consultation
   - ✲ Consultant as Negotiator/facilitator
   - ✲ Consultant as Collaborator
   - ✲ Process-oriented Consultant

2) Consultant-centered Consultation
   - ✲ Expert Consultant
   - ✲ Prescriptive Consultant
   - ✲ Trainer/educator

Theories of Consultation

- Person-centered Consultation
- Learning Theory
- Gestalt Consultation
- Psychoanalytic Approaches

The Counselor as Consultant

- Consultation and the College Counselor
- Consultation and the Community Agency Counselor
  - Consulting Outward
  - Consulting Inward
- The School Counselor as Consultant

Supervision

- A Systemic Perspective
- Who Is the Supervisor? The Supervisee?
- Individual or Group Supervision

Models of Supervision

(1) Developmental Models, (2) Orientation Specific, (3) Integrated

Supervision of Graduate Students

Supervision of Practicing Counselors

Multicultural Issues

- Multicultural Consultation Within a System
- Multicultural Consultation and Supervision with an Individual

Ethical, Professional, & Legal Issues

- Ethical Issues in Consultation
- Ethical Issues in Supervision
- Standards in Counseling Supervision
- Values in Consultation & Supervision
- Liability in Consultation & Supervision

The Counselor in Process: Committed to Ongoing Consultation and Supervision

SECTION IV:
THE DEVELOPMENT OF THE PERSON

Chapter 9: Development Across the Lifespan

Understanding Human Development

- Development Is Continual
- Development Is Orderly, Sequential, and Builds upon Itself
- Development Implies Change
- Development Is Growth-producing
- Developmental Models Are Transtheoretical
- Development Is Preventive, Optimistic, and Wellness-oriented

A Brief Overview of Physical and Psychosocial Development

- Development in Childhood
- Development in Adolescence and Adulthood

The Development of Knowing: Cognitive and Moral Changes

- Piaget's Stages of Cognitive Development
  - Preoperational Stage (Ages 2-7)
  - Concrete-operational Stage (Ages 7-11)
  - Formal-operational Stage (Ages 11-16)

- Kohlberg's Stages of Moral Development
  - Preconventional Level (Approx. Ages 2-7)
    - Stage 1- Avoidance of Punishment
    - Stage 2- Egocentric Hedonism
  - Conventional Level (Approx. Ages 8-13)
    - Stage 3- Social Conformity
    - Stage 4- Maintaining Rules, Law
  - Postconventional Level (Approx. Age 13+)
    - Stage 5- Choose Human Needs over Social Contract
    - Stage 6- Personal Conscience, Ethical Decision-making

- Gilligan's Stages of Women's Moral Development
  - Preconventional Level Girl
    - Narcissistic Reasoning; Functions from Self-protective Perspective
  - Conventional Level Woman
    - Puts Needs of Others Before Needs of Self
  - Postconventional Level
    - Balance Between Care/responsibility for Others and Self-care

- Comparison of Cognitive and Moral Development

<u>Adult Cognitive Development</u>

- Kegan's Constructive Developmental Model
  - Incorporative Stage
  - Impulsive Stage
  - Imperial Stage
  - Interpersonal Stage
  - Institutional Stage
  - Interindividual Stage

- Perry's Theory of Intellectual and Ethical Development
    - Dualism
    - Relativism
    - Commitment in Relativism

- Comparison of Adult Cognitive Development Theories

<u>Lifespan Development</u>

- Erikson's Stages of Psychosocial Development
    - Trust V. Mistrust (Birth to 1 Year)
    - Autonomy vs. Shame & Doubt (Ages 1-2)
    - Initiative vs. Guilt (Ages 3-5)
    - Industry vs. Inferiority (Ages 6-11)
    - Identity vs. Role Confusion (Adolescence)
    - Intimacy vs. Isolation (Early Adulthood)
    - Generativity vs. Stagnation (Middle Adulthood)
    - Integrity vs. Despair (Later Life)

- Levinson's Seasons of a Man's Life (Lifespan Approaches Cont'd)
  - Childhood & Adolescence
  - Early Adulthood
  - Middle Adulthood
  - Late Adulthood

<u>Comparison of Lifespan Development Theories</u>

<u>Fowler's Theory of Faith Development</u>

- Stage 0, Primary Faith (Infancy)
- Stage 1, Intuitive-projective Faith (Min. Age 4)
- Stage 2, Mythic-literal Faith (6 1/2 - 8)
- Stage 3, Synthetic-conventional Faith (12-13)
- Stage 4, Individuative-reflexive Faith (18-19)
- Stage 5, Paradoxical-conjunctive Faith (30-32)
- Age 6, Universalizing Faith (38-40)

<u>Other Developmental Theories</u>

Applying Knowledge of Development

Comparison of Developmental Models (see p. 248 of text)

Multicultural Issue: Development of Cultural Identity

Ethical, Professional, & Legal Issues

- ✲ ACA Code of Ethics: A Developmental Emphasis
- ✲ Professional Associations: AADA, C-AHEAD
- ✲ Missing Problems Because We're Too Positive

The Counselor in Process: Understanding Your Own Development

Chapter 10
Abnormal Development, Diagnosis, &

Why Study Abnormal Behavior, Diagnosis, and Medication?

Personality Development & Abnormal Behavior

- You Can't Have One Without the Other: Abnormal Behavior, Diagnosis, Medication
- Genetic and Biological Explanations
- Freud's Model of Psychosexual Development
- Learning Theory and the Development of the Person
- Humanistic Understanding of Personality Development

Diagnosis and Abnormal Behavior: What Is DSM-IV-TR?

- Five Axes
  - Axis I: All Disorders Except Personality Disorders or Mental Retardation
  - Axis II: Mental Retardation and Personality Disorders
  - Axis III: General Medical Conditions
  - Axis IV: Psychosocial/environmental Problems
  - Axis V: Global Assessment of Functioning

- Making a Diagnosis Using All Five Axes of DSM-IV-TR

Psychopharmacology

- Antipsychotics
- Antimanic Drugs
- Antidepressants
- Antianxiety Medications
- Stimulants

Multicultural Issue

- Misdiagnosis of Minority Clients
- Culture-bound Syndromes and DSM-IV-TR

Ethical, Professional, & Legal Issues

- Proper Diagnosis of Mental Disorders
- Challenges to the Concept of Abnormality
- Overdiagnosis of Mental Illness
- Confinement Against One's Will

The Counselor in Process: Dismissing Impaired Graduate Students

Chapter 11
Career Development

Defining Terms

- ✲ Avocation
- ✲ Career
- ✲ Career Awareness
- ✲ Career Development
- ✲ Career Counseling
- ✲ Career Guidance
- ✲ Career Path
- ✲ Jobs
- ✲ Leisure
- ✲ Occupation
- ✲ Work

Is Career Development Developmental?

A Little Bit of History

Theories of Career Development

- ✲ Trait-and-factor Approach
- ✲ Holland's Personality Theory
- ✲ Roe's Psychodynamic Theory
- ✲ Super's Lifespan Approach
- ✲ Cognitive Development Approaches
- ✲ Integrating Models

<u>The Use of Career-related Information</u>

- Occupational Classification Systems
  - Dictionary of Occupational Titles (DOT)
  - Guide for Occupational Exploration (GOE)
  - Occupational Outlook Handbook (OOH)

- Assessment Instruments
  - Interest Inventories
  - Assessment of Aptitude
  - Personality Assessment
  - Computer-assisted Career Guidance

<u>The Clinical Interview: The Lost Child in Career Development</u>

<u>Integrating Theory, Career Information, and Career Assessment</u>

<u>Multicultural Issues</u>

- Multicultural Career Counseling: Coming of Age
- Multicultural Theory of Career Development
- Career Counseling in a Diverse Culture

Ethical, Professional, & Legal Issues

- Ethical Standards for the Practice of Career Counseling and Consultation
- Competency Guidelines for Career Development
- Professional Associations in Career Development: NCDA and NECA

Optimizing Career Development (Optimizing Career Choices)

Legal Issues: Important Laws & Career Counseling

- Carl Perkins Act
- Americans with Disabilities Act
- PL94-142 (Education of All Handicapped Children Act)
- PL93-112
- Rehabilitation Act of 1973
- School-to-Work Opportunities Act
- Title VII and Title IX

The Counselor in Process: Career Development as a Lifespan Process

SECTION V: RESEARCH, PROGRAM EVALUATION, AND APPRAISAL

Chapter 12: Testing & Assessment

Why Testing?

A Little Background (History)

Types of Tests

- Formal Assessments
  - Assessment of Ability (Cognitive Realm)
    - Achievement Tests: 1) Survey, 2) Diagnostic, 3) Readiness
    - Aptitude Tests: 1) Individual Intelligence, 2) Cognitive Ability, 3) Special Aptitude, 4) Multiple Aptitude

- Personality Assessment (Affective Realm) (Formal Tests Cont'd)
  - Objective Personality Tests
  - Projective Tests
  - Interest Inventories

Types of Tests (Cont'd)

- Informal Assessments
  - Rating Scales
  - Numerical Scale
  - Likert-type Scale
  - Behavior Checklist
  - Rank Order
  - Observation

Test Categories

- Norm-referenced
- Criterion-referenced
- Standardized
- Nonstandardized

Test Statistics

- Relativity and Meaningfulness of Scores
- Measures of Central Tendency and Measures of Variability
- Derived Scores:
  - Percentiles
  - DIQ
  - Grade Equivalent
  - T-scores
  - SAT/GRE Type Scores
  - Stanines
  - Idiosyncratic Publisher Tests

Correlation Coefficient

What Makes a Good Test Good?

1) Validity
  - Face Validity
  - Criterion-related Validity
  - Content Validity
  - Construct Validity

2) Reliability
  - Test-retest Reliability
  - Split-half Reliability
  - Alternative Forms Reliability
  - Internal Consistency

What Makes a Good Test (Cont'd)

3) Practicality
4) Cross-cultural Fairness

Where to Find Tests

- Publisher Resource Catalogs
- Journals in the Field
- Source Books on Testing
- Experts
- The Internet

Writing Test Reports

Use of Computers in Testing

- Test Scoring and Reporting
- Administration of Tests
- Interpretation of Test Material
- Access to Tests on the Internet
- Increased Efficacy for the Testing of Individuals with Disabilities

Multicultural Issue: Caution in Using Tests

Ethical Issues in Testing

- ✲ Ethical and Technical Use of Tests
- ✲ Informed Consent
- ✲ Invasion of Privacy & Confidentiality
- ✲ Competence in Use of Tests
- ✲ Other Ethical Issues

Legal Issues: Laws That Impact Testing

- ✲ Buckley Amendment
- ✲ Freedom of Information Act
- ✲ PL94-142
- ✲ Carl Perkins Act (PL98-524)
- ✲ Americans with Disabilities Act
- ✲ Civil Rights Act ('64) & Amendments

The Counselor in Process: "Assessment of Clients"

Chapter 13
Research & Evaluation

The Purpose of Research

Two Types of Research

- Quantitative & Qualitative
- Literature Reviews (To Set up Study)

Research Designs

- Quantitative
  - Experimental Research
    - True Experimental Research
    - Quasi-experimental Research
    - Single-subject Designs
  - Nonexperimental Research
    - Correlational Research
    - Survey Research
    - Ex Post Facto (Causal-comparative)

- Qualitative
  - Ethnographic Research
    - Observation
    - Ethnographic Interviews
    - Documents and Artifact Collection
  - Historical Research
    - Oral Histories
    - Documents
    - Relics

<u>Statistics & Data Analysis</u>

- Quantitative Research: (1) Descriptive Statistics, (2) Inferential Statistics
- Qualitative Research: (1) Inductive Analysis, (2) Coding

<u>Issues of Quality in Research Studies</u>

- Internal Validity
- External Validity
- Is Validity Valid in Qualitative Research

<u>Reading & Writing Research</u>

- Abstract
- Review of the Literature
- Esearch Hypothesis
- Methodology
- Results
- Discussion, Implications, Conclusions
- References

<u>Program Evaluation</u>

- The Purpose of Evaluation

- Types of Evaluation
  - Formative Evaluation
  - Summative Evaluation

Multicultural Issues

- Bias in Research and Evaluation
- White Researchers Conducting Multicultural Research

Ethical, Professional, & Legal Issues

- Research Responsibilities
- Informed Consent
- Deception
- Confidentiality
- Standards in Research
- Exclusion of Females and Minorities in Research
- Institutional Review Boards

The Counselor in Process: Discovering New Paradigms

SECTION VI:
SOCIAL AND CULTURAL ISSUES IN COUNSELING

Chapter 14: Theory & Concepts of Multicultural Counseling

What Is Multicultural Counseling?

Why Multicultural Counseling?

- Diversity in America
- Counseling Is Not Working Many in U.s., Because:
- The Melting Pot Myth
- Incongruent Expectations about Counseling
- Lack of Understanding of Social Forces
- Ethnocentric Worldview
- Ignorance of Racist Attitudes & Prejudices
- Cultural Differences in Expression of Symptomatology
- Unreliability of Assessment/Research Instruments
- Institutional Racism

Some Definitions

- ✲ Culture
- ✲ Race
- ✲ Ethnicity
- ✲ Social Class
- ✲ Power Differentials
- ✲ Minority
- ✲ Stereotypes, Prejudice, & Racism
- ✲ Discrimination

Political Correctness: Or, Oh My God, What Do I Call Him or Her?

Conceptual Models for Working with Diverse Clients

- ✲ Minority Identity Models
  - ✲ Bell's Interpersonal Model
    - ✲ Aculturated Interpersonal Style
    - ✲ Bi-cultural Interpersonal Style
    - ✲ Culturally Immersed Interpersonal Style
    - ✲ Traditional Interpersonal Style

- Atkinson's Developmental Model (Minority Identity Models Cont'd)
  - Stage 1: Conformity
  - Stage 2: Dissonance
  - Stage 3: Resistance and Immersion
  - Stage 4: Introspection
  - Stage 5: Synergetic Articulation and Awareness

- White Identity Model: Sabnani, et al. Stages of White Identity Development
  - Stage 1: Pre-exposure
  - Stage 2: Exposure
  - Stage 3: Prominority/antiracism
  - Stage 4: Retreat to White Culture
  - Stage 5: Redefinition & Integration

<u>The Helping Relationship & Cultural Diversity</u>

- The Culturally-skilled Counselor
  - Attitudes and Beliefs
  - Knowledge
  - Skills

Multicultural Issue: Multicultural Counseling as the "Fourth Force"

Ethical, Professional, & Legal Trends

- Increasing Emphasis on Multicultural Standards
- Training in Multicultural Counseling
- Association for Multicultural Counseling & Development (AMCD)
- Knowledge of Legal Trends

The Counselor in Process: Working with Culturally Different Clients

Chapter 15
Knowledge & Skills of Multicultural Counseling

The Changing Face of America

- Changing Immigration Patterns
- See Figure 15.1 in Text

Understanding and Counseling Select Culturally Diverse Groups

- People from Varying Cultural/Racial Heritages
  - African Americans
  - People of Asian & Pacific Island origin
  - Hispanic peoples
  - Native Americans
  - Counseling Individuals from Different Cultures

- Religious Diversity in America
  - Christianity
  - Islam
  - Buddhism
  - Judaism
  - Hinduism
  - Counseling Individuals from Diverse Religious Backgrounds

- Gender Differences in America
  - Counseling Women
  - Counseling Men
  - Counseling Men and Women: A Final Viewpoint

- Differences in Sexual Orientation
  - Counseling Gay Men & Lesbian Women

- Other Populations
  - HIV Positive Individuals
    - Counseling Individuals Who Are HIV Positive
  - The Hungry, Homeless, and Poor
    - Counseling the Hungry, the Homeless, and the Poor
  - Older Persons
    - Counseling Older Persons
  - The Mentally Ill
    - Counseling the Chronically Mentally Ill
  - People with Disabilities
    - Counseling People with Disabilities

Multicultural Issue: Is all Counseling Multicultural?

Ethical, Professional, and Legal Issues

* Making Wise Ethical Decision: Limitations of Ethical Codes When Dealing with Diversity

The Counselor in Process: The Ongoing Process of Counseling the Culturally Different

SECTION VII:
YOUR FUTURE IN THE COUNSELING PROFESSION: CHOOSING A SPECIALTY AREA, FINDING A JOB, AND TRENDS IN THE FUTURE

Chapter 16: School Counseling

What Is School Counseling?

History of School Counseling

Roles and Functions of School Counselors

- Large Group Guidance
- Individual & Group Counseling
- Consultation
- Coordination

Theory & Process of School Counseling

- Comprehensive Developmental School Guidance and Counseling
  1) Planning the Program
  2) Designing the Program
  3) Implementing the Program

Where Do You Find School Counselors? (And, How Are They Different?)

- Elementary School Counselors
- Middle School Counselors
- Secondary School Counselors

Special Issues in School Counseling

- Transforming School Counseling in the 21st Century
- National Standards for School Counseling Programs
    - Academic Development
    - Career Development
    - Personal/social Development
- Working with Troubled Youth

Professional Development for School Counselors

Salaries & Job Outlook of School Counselors

Multicultural Issues: Creating a Multicultural School Environment

Ethical, Professional, and Legal Issues

- Ethical Issues
  - ASCAs Code of Ethics
  - Tips for Counselors

- Professional Issues
  - ASCA: in or out of ACA
  - Specialty Certifications in School Counseling

- Select Legal Issues
- Confidentiality, Privileged Communication, and the Law
- Child's Right to Confidentiality/parents' Right to Confidential Info
- PL94-142, Idea, Section 504, & the ADA
- Parental Rights to School Records (FERPA)
- Reporting Suspected Child Abuse
- The Hatch Amendment

The School Counselor in Process: Adapting to the 21st Century

Chapter 17
Community Agency Counseling

What Are Community Agency and Mental Health Counseling?

History of Community Agency and Mental Health Counseling

Where Do You Find Community Agency Counselors?

- Community Mental Health Centers
- Youth Services Programs
- Rehabilitation Agencies
- Private Practice Settings
- HMOs, PPOs, and EAPs
- Gerontological Settings
- Substance Abuse Settings
- Correctional Facilities
- Family Service Agencies
- Employment Agencies
- The Military
- Residential Treatment Centers
- Pastoral & Religious Settings
- Other Settings

Roles & Functions of Community Agency Counselors

- Case Manager
- Appraiser of Client Needs
- Counselor
- Consultant
- Supervisor/supervisee
- Professional Who Is Accountable
- Other Roles (e.g., 13 as identified by SREB)

Theory and Process of Agency/Mental Health Counselors

Special Issues in Community Agency Counseling

- Changes in the health care delivery system
- Deinstitutionalization
- DSM-IV-TR
- Psychotropic medication

Salaries & Job Outlook of Agency/Mental Health Counselors

Multicultural Issues

- Broad issues Hindering Multicultural Counseling at Agencies
- Assessment of clients
- Limited number of Minority Counselors

Professional, Ethical, and Legal Issues

- Ethical Complaints Made Against Licensed Professional Counselors
- Professional Associations
- Credentialing

The Agency/Mental Health Counselor in Process: Growing, Changing, Accepting

Chapter 18
Student Affairs Practice in Higher Education

What Is Student Affairs?

History of Student Affairs

Where Do You Find Student Affairs Counselors?

- Campus Counseling Center
- Career Development Services
- Residence Life and Housing Services
- Office of Disability Services
- Multicultural Student Services
- Student Activities Services
- Office of Human Resources
- Academic Support Services
- Other Student Services Offices

Roles & Functions of Student Affairs Specialists

- The Administrator
- The Counselor
- The Educator
- The Campus Ecology Manager

Theories of Student Development

✲ Chickering's 7 Vectors of Student Development

1) Achieving Competence
2) Managing Emotions
3) Developing Autonomy
4) Establishing Identity
5) Freeing Interpersonal Relationships
6) Developing Purpose
7) Developing Integrity

✲ Perry's Scheme of Intellectual & Ethical Development

1) Dualism
2) Relativism
3) Commitment in Relativism

✲ Other Theories of Development

Special Issues in Student Development Counseling

- Barriers to Academic Excellence of Under-represented Students
- "In Loco Parentis": A New View
- Defining the Role of Student Affairs Practice

Salaries of Student Affairs Practitioners

Multicultural Issues

- Addressing the Student/faculty Barrier
- Applying Student Development Theory to Minority Students
- Implementing a Cultural Environment Transitions Model
- Becoming a Cultural Broker

Ethical & Professional Issues for the Student Affairs Practitioner

- Ethical Concerns
  - Ethical Guidelines
  - Confidentiality and Duty to Warn
  - Confidentiality, Informed Consent, and the Breaking of Rules

✲ Professional Issue: Diversity of the Profession

✲ Legal Issue: Liability Concerns

- ✲ Negligence
- ✲ Alcohol Abuse
- ✲ Defamation and Libel
- ✲ Civil Rights Liability
- ✲ Contract Liability
- ✲ The Buckley Amendment (FERPA)

<u>The Counselor in Process: The Student Affairs Practitioner</u>

Chapter 19
A Look Toward The Future

Medical Breakthroughs (1) Genetic Research and Genetic Counseling, (2) Psychotropic Medications, (3) The Mind Body Connection

HMOs, PPOs, Uh Oh, and the Changing Nature of Therapeutic Practice

Computers and the Information Superhighway

Your Future: Choosing a Counseling Program/Finding a Job

- Know Where You're Applying
- Know and Adhere to the Application Process
- The Resume
- Preparing a Portfolio
- Locating a Graduate Program/Finding a Job
- Finding a Graduate Program
- Finding a Job

- Networking (Choosing a Counseling Program/Finding a Job Cont'd)
- Going on Informational Interviews
- Responding to Ads in Professional Publications
- Interviewing at National Conferences
- College and University Job Placement Services
- Other Job Finding Methods
- Being Chosen, Being Rejected

Multicultural Issue: Increased Emphasis on Multicultural Counseling

Ethical, Professional, and Legal Issues: The Future?

- Expansion of Accreditation
- Proliferation of Credentials
- Increased Emphasis on Standards of Care
- After Changes Upon Changes We Are More Or Less the Same
- A Wellness Model for Counselors

The Counselor in Process: Remaining Behind or Moving Forward